YOUR PERSONAL
HOROSCOPE
2017

ARIES

D1143870

YOUR PERSONAL HOROSCOPE 2017

ARIES

21st March–20th April

igloobooks

igloobooks

Published in 2016
by Igloo Books Ltd
Cottage Farm
Sywell
NN6 0BJ
www.igloobooks.com

Produced for Igloo Books by Foulsham Publishing Ltd, The Old Barrel Store,
Drayman's Lane, Marlow, Bucks SL7 2FF, England

FIR003 0716
2 4 6 8 10 9 7 5 3 1
ISBN: 978-1-78557-504-4

This is an abridged version of material originally published
in Old Moore's Horoscope and Astral Diary.

Cover images: iStock
Cover designed by Nicholas Gage

Printed and manufactured in China

CONTENTS

INTRODUCTION

Your Personal Horoscopes have been specifically created to allow you to get the most from astrological patterns and the way they have a bearing on not only your zodiac sign, but nuances within it. Using the diary section of the book you can read about the influences and possibilities of each and every day of the year. It will be possible for you to see when you are likely to be cheerful and happy or those times when your nature is in retreat and you will be more circumspect. The diary will help to give you a feel for the specific 'cycles' of astrology and the way they can subtly change your day-to-day life. For example, when you see the sign ☿, this means that the planet Mercury is retrograde at that time. Retrograde means it appears to be running backwards through the zodiac. Such a happening has a significant effect on communication skills, but this is only one small aspect of how the Personal Horoscope can help you.

With Your Personal Horoscope the story doesn't end with the diary pages. It includes simple ways for you to work out the zodiac sign the Moon occupied at the time of your birth, and what this means for your personality. In addition, if you know the time of day you were born, it is possible to discover your Ascendant, yet another important guide to your personal make-up and potential.

Many readers are interested in relationships and in knowing how well they get on with people of other astrological signs. You might also be interested in the way you appear to very different sorts of individuals. If you are such a person, the section on Venus will be of particular interest. Despite the rapidly changing position of this planet, you can work out your Venus sign, and learn what bearing it will have on your life.

Using Your Personal Horoscope you can travel on one of the most fascinating and rewarding journeys that anyone can take – the journey to a better realisation of self.

THE ESSENCE OF ARIES

Exploring the Personality of Aries the Ram

(21ST MARCH–20TH APRIL)

What's in a sign?

Aries is not the first sign of the zodiac by accident. It's the place in the year when the spring begins, and so it represents some of the most dynamic forces in nature, and within the zodiac as a whole. As a result the very essence of your nature is geared towards promoting yourself in life and pushing your ideas forward very positively. You don't accept a great deal of interference in your life, but you are quite willing to help others as much as you can, provided that to do so doesn't curb your natural desire to get on in life.

Aries people are not universally liked, though your true friends remain loyal to you under almost any circumstances. But why should it be that such a dynamic and go-getting person does meet with some opposition? The answer is simple: not everyone is quite so sure of themselves as you are and many tend to get nervous when faced with the sheer power of the Aries personality. If there is one factor within your own control that could counter these problems it is the adoption of some humility – that commodity which is so important for you to dredge from the depths of your nature. If you only show the world that you are human, and that you are well aware of the fact, most people would follow you willingly to the very gates of hell. The most successful Aries subjects know this fact and cultivate it to the full.

Your executive skills are never in doubt and you can get almost anything practical done whilst others are still jumping from foot to foot. That's why you are such a good organiser and are so likely to be out there at the front of any venture. Adventurous and quite willing to show your bravery in public, you can even surprise yourself sometimes with the limits you are likely to go to in order to reach solutions that seem right to you.

Kind to those you take to, you can be universally loved when working at your best. Despite this there will be times in your life when you simply can't understand why some people just don't like you. Maybe there's an element of jealousy involved.

Aries resources

The part of the zodiac occupied by the sign of Aries has, for many centuries, been recognised as the home of self-awareness. This means that there isn't a person anywhere else in the zodiac that has a better knowledge of self than you do. But this isn't necessarily an intellectual process with Aries, more a response to the very blood that is coursing through your veins. Aries' success doesn't so much come from spending hours working out the pros and cons of any given course of action, more from the thrill of actually getting stuck in. If you find yourself forced into a life that means constantly having to think everything through to the tiniest detail, there is likely to be some frustration in evidence.

Aries is ruled by Mars, arguably the most go-getting of all the planets in the solar system. Mars is martial and demands practical ways of expressing latent power. It also requires absolute obedience from subordinates. When this is forthcoming, Aries individuals are the most magnanimous people to be found anywhere. Loyalty is not a problem and there have been many instances in history when Aries people were quite willing to die for their friends if necessary.

When other people are willing to give up and go with the flow, you will still be out there pitching for the result that seems most advantageous to you. It isn't something you can particularly control and those who don't know you well could find you sometimes curt and over-demanding as a result. But because you are tenacious you can pick the bones out of any situation and will usually arrive at your desired destination, if you don't collapse with fatigue on the way.

Routines, or having to take life at the pace of less motivated types, won't suit you at all. Imprisonment of any sort, even in a failed relationship, is sheer torture and you will move heaven and earth to get out into the big, wide world, where you can exploit your natural potential to the full. Few people know you really well because you don't always explain yourself adequately. The ones who do adore you.

Beneath the surface

Whereas some zodiac signs are likely to spend a great deal of their lives looking carefully at the innermost recesses of their own minds, Aries individuals tend to prefer the cut and thrust of the practical world. Aries people are not natural philosophers, but that doesn't mean that you aren't just as complicated beneath the surface as any of your astrological brothers and sisters. So what is it that makes the Aries firebrand think and act in the way that it does? To a great extent it is a lack of basic self-confidence.

This statement might seem rather odd, bearing in mind that a fair percentage of the people running our world were born under the sign of the Ram, but it is true nevertheless. Why? Because people who know themselves and their capabilities really well don't feel the constant need to prove themselves in the way that is the driving force of your zodiac sign. Not that your naturally progressive tendencies are a fault. On the contrary, if used correctly they can help you to create a much better, fairer and happier world, at least in your own vicinity.

The fact that you occasionally take your ball and go home if you can't get your own way is really down to the same insecurity that is noticeable through many facets of your nature. If Aries can't rule, it often doesn't want to play at all. A deep resentment and a brooding quality can build up in the minds and souls of some thwarted Aries types, a tendency that you need to combat. Better by far to try and compromise, itself a word that doesn't exist in the vocabularies of the least enlightened people born under the sign of the Ram. Once this lesson is learned, inner happiness increases and you relax into your life much more.

The way you think about others is directly related to the way you consider they think about you. This leads to another surprising fact regarding the zodiac sign. Aries people absolutely hate to be disliked, though they would move heaven and earth to prove that this isn't the case. And as a result Aries both loves and hates with a passion. Deep inside you can sometimes be a child shivering in the dark. If you only realise this fact your path to happiness and success is almost assured. Of course to do so takes a good deal of courage – but that's a commodity you don't lack.

11

Making the best of yourself

It would be quite clear to any observer that you are not the sort of person who likes to hang around at the back of a queue, or who would relish constantly taking orders from people who may not know situations as well as you do. For that reason alone you are better in positions that see you out there at the front, giving commands and enjoying the cut and thrust of everyday life. In a career sense this means that whatever you do you are happiest telling those around you how to do it too. Many Aries people quite naturally find their way to the top of the tree and don't usually have too much trouble staying there.

It is important to remember, however, that there is another side to your nature: the giving qualities beneath your natural dominance. You can always be around when people need you the most, encouraging and even gently pushing when it is necessary. By keeping friends and being willing to nurture relationships across a broad spectrum, you gradually get to know what makes those around you tick. This makes for a more patient and understanding sort of Aries subject – the most potent of all.

Even your resilience is not endless, which is why it is important to remember that there are times when you need rest. Bearing in mind that you are not superhuman is the hardest lesson to learn, but the admission brings humility, something that Aries needs to cultivate whenever possible.

Try to avoid living a restricted life and make your social contacts frequent and important. Realise that there is much more to life than work and spend some of your free time genuinely attempting to help those who are less well off than you are. Crucially you must remember that 'help' is not the same as domination.

The impressions you give

This section may well be of less interest to Aries subjects than it would be to certain other zodiac signs. The reason is quite clear. Aries people are far less interested in what others think about them than almost anyone else – or at least they tell themselves that they are. Either way it is counterproductive to ignore the opinions of the world at large because to do so creates stumbling blocks, even in a practical sense.

Those around you probably find you extremely capable and well able to deal with almost any situation that comes your way. Most are willing to rely heavily on you and the majority would almost instinctively see you as a leader. Whether or not they like you at the same time is really dependent on the way you handle situations. That's the difference between the go-getting, sometimes selfish type of Aries subject and the more enlightened amongst this illustrious sign.

You are viewed as being exciting and well able to raise enthusiasm for almost any project that takes your fancy. Of course this implies a great responsibility because you are always expected to come up with the goods. The world tends to put certain people on a pedestal, and you are one of them. On the other side of the coin we are all inclined to fire arrows at the elevated, so maintaining your position isn't very easy.

Most of the time you are seen as being magnanimous and kind, factors that you can exploit, whilst at the same time recognising the depth of the responsibility that comes with being an Aries subject. It might not be a bad thing to allow those around you to see that you too have feet of clay. This will make them respect and support you all the more, and even Aries people really do need to feel loved. A well-balanced Aries subject is one of the most elevated spirits to be found anywhere.

The way forward

You certainly enjoy life more when looking at it from the top of the tree. Struggling to get by is not in the least interesting to your zodiac sign and you can soon become miserable if things are not going well for you. That's why it is probably quite justified in your case to work tenaciously in order to achieve your objectives. Ideally, once you have realised some sort of success and security for yourself, you should then be willing to sit and watch life go by a little more. In fact this doesn't happen. The reason for this is clear. The Aries subject who learns how to succeed rarely knows when to stop – it's as simple as that.

Splitting your life into different components can help, if only because this means that you don't get the various elements mixed up. So, for example, don't confuse your love life with your professional needs, or your family with colleagues. This process allows you to view life in manageable chunks and also makes it possible for you to realise when any one of them may be working well. As a result you will put the effort where it's needed, and enjoy what is going well for you.

If you want to know real happiness you will also have to learn that acquisition for its own sake brings hollow rewards at best. When your talents are being turned outward to the world at large, you are one of the most potent and successful people around. What is more you should find yourself to be a much happier person when you are lending a hand to the wider world. This is possible, maybe outside of your normal professional sphere, though even where voluntary work is concerned it is important not to push yourself to the point of fatigue.

Keep yourself physically fit, without necessarily expecting that you can run to the South Pole and back, and stay away from too many stimulants, such as alcohol and nicotine. The fact is that you are best when living a healthy life, but it doesn't help either if you make even abstinence into an art form. Balance is important, as is moderation – itself a word that is difficult for you to understand. In terms of your approach to other people it's important to realise that everyone has a specific point of view. These might be different to yours, but they are not necessarily wrong. Sort out the friends who are most important to you and stick with them, whilst at the same time realising that almost everyone can be a pal – with just a little effort.

ARIES ON THE CUSP

Astrological profiles are altered for those people born at either the beginning or the end of a zodiac sign, or, more properly, on the cusps of a sign. In the case of Aries this would be on the 21st of March and for two or three days after, and similarly at the end of the sign, probably from the 18th to the 20th of April.

The Pisces Cusp – 21st March to 24th March

With the Sun so close to the zodiac sign of Pisces at the time you were born, it is distinctly possible that you have always had some doubts when reading a character breakdown written specifically for the sign of Aries. This isn't surprising because no zodiac sign has a definite start or end, they merely merge together. As a result there are some of the characteristics of the sign of the Fishes that are intermingled with the qualities of Aries in your nature.

What we probably find, as a result, is a greater degree of emotional sensitivity and a tendency to be more cognisant of what the rest of humanity is feeling. This is not to imply that Aries is unfeeling, but rather that Pisceans actively make humanity their business.

You are still able to achieve your most desired objectives in the practical world, but on the way, you stop to listen to the heartbeat of the planet on which you live. A very good thing, of course, but at the same time there is some conflict created if your slightly dream-like tendencies get in the way of your absolute need to see things through to their logical conclusion.

Nobody knows you better than you know yourself, or at least that's what the Aries qualities within you say, but that isn't always verified by some of the self-doubt that comes from the direction of the Fishes. As in all matters astrological, a position of balance has to be achieved in order to reconcile the differing qualities of your nature. In your case, this is best accomplished by being willing to stop and think once in a while and by refusing to allow your depth to be a problem.

Dealt with properly, the conjoining of Pisces and Aries can be a wondrous and joyful affair, a harmony of opposites that always makes you interesting to know. Your position in the world is naturally one of authority but at the same time you need to serve. That's why some people with this sort of mixture of astrological qualities would make such good administrators in a hospital, or in any position where the alternate astrological needs are well balanced. In the chocolate box of life you are certainly a 'soft centre'.

The Taurus Cusp – 18th April to 20th April

The merge from Aries to Taurus is much less well defined than the one at the other side of Aries, but it can be very useful to you all the same. Like the Pisces-influenced Aries you may be slightly more quiet than would be the case with the Ram taken alone and your thought processes are probably not quite as fast. But to compensate for this fact you don't rush into things quite as much and are willing to allow ideas to mature more fully.

Your sense of harmony and beauty is strong and you know, in a very definite way, exactly what you want. As a result your home will be distinctive but tasteful and it's a place where you need space to be alone sometimes, which the true Aries subject probably does not. You do not lack the confidence to make things look the way you want them, but you have a need to display these things to the world at large and sometimes even to talk about how good you are at decoration and design.

If anyone finds you pushy, it is probably because they don't really know what makes you tick. Although you are willing to mix with almost anyone, you are more inclined, at base, to have a few very close friends who stay at the forefront of your life for a long time. It is likely that you enjoy refined company and you wouldn't take kindly to the dark, the sordid, or the downright crude in life.

Things don't get you down as much as can sometimes be seen to be the case for Taurus when taken alone and you are rarely stumped for a progressive and practical idea when one is needed most. At all levels, your creative energy is evident and some of you even have the ability to make this into a business, since Aries offers the practical and administrative spark that Taurus can sometimes lack.

In matters of love, you are ardent and sincere, probably an idealist, and you know what you want in a partner. Whilst this is also true in the case of Taurus, you are different, because you are much more likely, not only to look, but also to say something about the way you feel.

Being naturally friendly you rarely go short of the right sort of help and support when it is most vital. Part of the reason for this lies in the fact that you are so willing to be the sounding-board for the concerns of your friends. All in all you can be very contented with your lot, but you never stop searching for something better all the same. At its best, this is one of the most progressive cuspal matches of them all.

ARIES AND ITS ASCENDANTS

The nature of every individual on the planet is composed of the rich variety of zodiac signs and planetary positions that were present at the time of their birth. Your Sun sign, which in your case is Aries, is one of the many factors when it comes to assessing the unique person you are. Probably the most important consideration, other than your Sun sign, is to establish the zodiac sign that was rising over the eastern horizon at the time that you were born. This is your Ascending or Rising sign. Most popular astrology fails to take account of the Ascendant, and yet its importance remains with you from the very moment of your birth, through every day of your life. The Ascendant is evident in the way you approach the world, and so, when meeting a person for the first time, it is this astrological influence that you are most likely to notice first. Our Ascending sign essentially represents what we appear to be, while our Sun sign is what we feel inside ourselves.

The Ascendant also has the potential for modifying our overall nature. For example, if you were born at a time of day when Aries was passing over the eastern horizon (this would be around the time of dawn) then you would be classed as a double Aries. As such you would typify this zodiac sign, both internally and in your dealings with others. However, if your Ascendant sign turned out to be a Water sign, such as Pisces, there would be a profound alteration of nature, away from the expected qualities of Aries.

One of the reasons that popular astrology often ignores the Ascendant is that it has always been rather difficult to establish. We have found a way to make this possible by devising an easy-to-use table, which you will find on page 157 of this book. Using this, you can establish your Ascendant sign at a glance. You will need to know your rough time of birth, then it is simply a case of following the instructions.

For those readers who have no idea of their time of birth it might be worth allowing a good friend, or perhaps your partner, to read through the section that follows this introduction. Someone who deals with you on a regular basis may easily discover your Ascending sign, even though you could have some difficulty establishing it for yourself. A good understanding of this component of your nature is essential if you want to be aware of that 'other person' who is responsible for the way you make contact with the world at large. Your Sun sign, Ascendant sign, and the other pointers in this book will, together, allow you a far better understanding of what makes you tick as an individual. Peeling back the different layers of your astrological make-up can be an enlightening experience, and the Ascendant may represent one of the most important layers of all.

Aries with Aries Ascendant

What you see is what you get with this combination. You typify the no-nonsense approach of Aries at its best. All the same this combination is quite daunting when viewed through the eyes of other, less dominant sorts of people. You tend to push your way though situations that would find others cowering in a corner and you are afraid of very little. With a determination to succeed that makes you a force to be reckoned with, you leave the world in no doubt as to your intentions and tend to be rather too brusque for your own good on occasions.

At heart you are kind and loving, able to offer assistance to the downtrodden and sad, and usually willing to take on board the cares of people who have a part to play in your life. No-one would doubt your sincerity, or your honesty, though you may utilise slightly less than orthodox ways of getting your own way on those occasions when you feel you have right on your side. You are a loving partner and a good parent, though where children are concerned you tend to be rather too protective. The trouble is that you know what a big, bad world it can be and probably feel that you are better equipped to deal with things than anyone else.

Aries with Taurus Ascendant

This is a much quieter combination, so much so that even experienced astrologers would be unlikely to recognise you as an Aries subject at all, unless of course they came to know you very well. Your approach to life tends to be quiet and considered and there is a great danger that you could suppress those feelings that others of your kind would be only too willing to verbalise. To compensate you are deeply creative and will think matters through much more readily than more dominant Aries types would be inclined to do. Reaching out towards the world, you are, nevertheless, somewhat locked inside yourself and can struggle to achieve the level of communication that you so desperately need. Frustration might easily follow, were it not for the fact that you possess a quiet determination that, to those in the know, is the clearest window through to your Aries soul.

The care for others is stronger here than with almost any other Aries type and you certainly demonstrate this at all levels. The fact is that you live a great percentage of your life in service to the people you take to, whilst at the same time being able to shut the door firmly in the face of people who irritate or anger you. You are deeply motivated towards family relationships.

Aries with Gemini Ascendant

A fairly jolly combination this, though by no means easy for others to come to terms with. You fly about from pillar to post and rarely stop long enough to take a breath. Admittedly this suits your own needs very well, but it can be a source of some disquiet to those around you, since they may not possess your energy or motivation. Those who know you well are deeply in awe of your capacity to keep going long after almost everyone else would have given up and gone home, though this quality is not always as wonderful as it sounds because it means that you put more pressure on your nervous system than just about any other astrological combination.

You need to be mindful of your nervous system, which responds to the erratic, mercurial quality of Gemini. Problems only really arise when the Aries part of you makes demands that the Gemini component finds difficult to deal with. There are paradoxes galore here and some of them need sorting out if you are ever fully to understand yourself, or are to be in a position when others know what makes you tick.

In relationships you might be a little fickle, but you are a real charmer and never stuck for the right words, no matter who you are dealing with. Your tenacity knows no bounds, though perhaps it should!

Aries with Cancer Ascendant

The main problem that you experience in life shows itself as a direct result of the meshing of these two very different zodiac signs. At heart Aries needs to dominate, whereas Cancer shows a desire to nurture. All too often the result can be a protective arm that is so strong that nobody could possibly get out from under it. Lighten your own load, and that of those you care for, by being willing to sit back and watch others please themselves a little. You might think that you know best, and your heart is clearly in the right place, but try to realise what life is like when someone is always on hand to tell you that they know better then you do.

But in a way this is a little severe, because you are fairly intuitive and your instincts would rarely lead you astray. Nobody could ask for a better partner or parent than you, though they might request a slightly less attentive one. In matters of work you are conscientious and are probably best suited to a job that means sorting out the kind of mess that humanity is so good at creating. You probably spend your spare time untangling balls of wool, though you are quite sporting too and could easily make the Olympics. Once there you would not win however, because you would be too concerned about all the other competitors.

Aries with Leo Ascendant

Here we come upon the first situation of Aries being allied with another Fire sign. This creates a character that could appear to be typically Aries at first sight and in many ways it is, though there are subtle differences that should not be ignored. Although you have the typical Aries ability to get things done, many of the tasks you do undertake will be for and on behalf of others. You can be proud, and on some occasions even haughty, and yet you are also regal in your bearing and honest to the point of absurdity. Nobody could doubt your sincerity and you have the soul of a poet combined with the courage of a lion.

All this is good, but it makes you rather difficult to approach, unless the person in question has first adopted a crouching and subservient attitude although you would not wish them to do so. It's simply that the impression you give and the motivation that underpins it are two quite different things. You are greatly respected and in the case of those individuals who know your real nature, you are also deeply loved. But life would be much simpler if you didn't always have to fight the wars that those around you are happy to start. Relaxation is a word that you don't really understand and you would do yourself a favour if you looked it up in a dictionary.

Aries with Virgo Ascendant

Virgo is steady and sure, though also fussy and stubborn. Aries is fast and determined, restless and active. It can already be seen that this is a rather strange meeting of characteristics and because Virgo is ruled by the capricious Mercury, the ultimate result will change from hour to hour and day to day. It isn't merely that others find it difficult to know where they are with you, they can't even understand what makes you tick. This will make you the subject of endless fascination and attention, at which you will be apparently surprised but inwardly pleased. If anyone ever really gets to know what goes on in that busy mind they may find the implications very difficult to deal with and it is a fact that only you would have the ability to live inside your crowded head.

As a partner and a parent you are second to none, though you tend to get on better with your children once they start to grow, since by this time you may be slightly less restricting to their own desires, which will often clash with your own on their behalf. You are capable of give and take and could certainly not be considered selfish, though your constant desire to get the best from everyone might occasionally be misconstrued.

Aries with Libra Ascendant

Libra has the tendency to bring out the best in any zodiac sign, and this is no exception when it comes together with Aries. You may, in fact, be the most comfortable of all Aries types, simply because Libra tempers some of your more assertive qualities and gives you the chance to balance out opposing forces, both inside yourself and in the world outside. You are fun to be with and make the staunchest friend possible. Although you are generally affable, few people would try to put one over on you, because they would quickly come to know how far you are willing to go before you let forth a string of invective that would shock those who previously underestimated your basic Aries traits.

Home and family are very dear to you, but you are more tolerant than some Aries types are inclined to be and you have a youthful zest for life that should stay with you no matter what age you manage to achieve. There is always something interesting to do and your mind is a constant stream of possibilities. This makes you very creative and you may also demonstrate a desire to look good at all times. You may not always be quite as confident as you appear to be, but few would guess the fact.

Aries with Scorpio Ascendant

The two very different faces of Mars come together in this potent, magnetic and quite awe-inspiring combination. Your natural inclination is towards secrecy and this fact, together with the natural attractions of the sensual Scorpio nature, makes you the object of great curiosity. This means that you will not go short of attention and should ensure that you are always being analysed by people who may never get to know you at all. At heart you prefer your own company, and yet life appears to find means to push you into the public gaze time and again. Most people with this combination ooze sex appeal and can use this fact as a stepping stone to personal success, yet without losing any integrity or loosening the cords of a deeply moralistic nature.

On those occasions when you do lose your temper, there isn't a character in the length and breadth of the zodiac who would have either the words or the courage to stand against the stream of invective that follows. On really rare occasions you might even scare yourself. As far as family members are concerned a simple look should be enough to show when you are not amused. Few people are left unmoved by your presence in their life.

Aries with Sagittarius Ascendant

What a lovely combination this can be, for the devil-may-care aspects of Sagittarius lighten the load of a sometimes too-serious Aries interior. Everything that glistens is not gold, though it's hard to convince you of the fact because, to mix metaphors, you can make a silk purse out of a sow's ear. Almost everyone loves you and in return you offer a friendship that is warm and protective, but not as demanding as sometimes tends to be the case with the Aries type. Relationships may be many and varied and there is often more than one major attachment in the life of those holding this combination. You will bring a breath of spring to any attachment, though you need to ensure that the person concerned is capable of keeping up with the hectic pace of your life.

It may appear from time to time that you are rather too trusting for your own good, though deep inside you are very astute and it seems that almost everything you undertake works out well in the end. This has nothing to do with native luck and is really down to the fact that you are much more calculating than might appear to be the case at first sight. As a parent you are protective yet offer sufficient room for self-expression.

Aries with Capricorn Ascendant

If ever anyone could be accused of setting off immediately, but slowly, it has to be you. These are very contradictory signs and the differences will express themselves in a variety of ways. One thing is certain, you have tremendous tenacity and will see a job through patiently from beginning to end, without tiring on the way, and ensuring that every detail is taken care of properly. This combination often bestows good health and a great capacity for continuity, particularly in terms of the length of life. You are certainly not as argumentative as the typical Aries, but you do know how to get your own way, which is just as well because you are usually thinking on behalf of everyone else and not just on your own account.

At home you can relax, which is a blessing for Aries, though in fact you seldom choose to do so because you always have some project or other on the go. You probably enjoy knocking down and rebuilding walls, though this is a practical tendency and not responsive to relationships, in which you are ardent and sincere. Impetuosity is as close to your heart as is the case for any type of Aries subject, though you certainly have the ability to appear patient and steady. But it's just a front, isn't it?

Aries with Aquarius Ascendant

The person standing on a soap box in the corner of the park, extolling the virtues of this or that, could quite easily be an Aries with an Aquarian Ascendant. You are certainly not averse to speaking your mind and you have plenty to talk about because you are the best social reformer and political animal of them all. Unorthodox in your approach, you have the ability to keep everyone guessing, except when it comes to getting your own way, for in this nobody doubts your natural abilities. You can put theories into practice very well and on the way you retain a sense of individuality that would shock more conservative types. It's true that a few people might find you a little difficult to approach and this is partly because you have an inner reserve and strength which is difficult for others to fathom.

In the world at large you take your place at the front, as any good Arian should, and yet you offer room for others to share your platform. You keep up with the latest innovations and treat family members as the genuine friends that you believe them to be. Care needs to be taken when picking a life partner, for you are an original, and not just anyone could match the peculiarities thrown up by this astrological combination.

Aries with Pisces Ascendant

Although not an easy combination to deal with, the Aries with a Piscean Ascendant does, nevertheless, bring something very special to the world in the way of natural understanding allied to practical assistance. It's true that you can sometimes be a dreamer, but there is nothing wrong with that as long as you have the ability to turn some of your wishes into reality, and this you are easily able to do, usually for the sake of those around you. Conversation comes easily to you, though you also possess a slightly wistful and poetic side to your nature, which is attractive to the many people who call you a friend. A natural entertainer, you bring a sense of the comic to the often serious qualities of Aries, though without losing the determination that typifies the sign.

In relationships you are ardent, sincere and supportive, with a strong social conscience that sometimes finds you fighting the battles of the less privileged members of society. Family is important to you and this is a combination that invariably leads to parenthood. Away from the cut and thrust of everyday life you relax more fully and think about matters more deeply than more typical Aries types might.

THE MOON AND THE PART IT PLAYS IN YOUR LIFE

In astrology the Moon is probably the single most important heavenly body after the Sun. Its unique position, as partner to the Earth on its journey around the solar system, means that the Moon appears to pass through the signs of the zodiac extremely quickly. The zodiac position of the Moon at the time of your birth plays a great part in personal character and is especially significant in the build-up of your emotional nature.

Your Own Moon Sign

Discovering the position of the Moon at the time of your birth has always been notoriously difficult because tracking the complex zodiac positions of the Moon is not easy. This process has been reduced to three simple stages with our Lunar Tables. A breakdown of the Moon's zodiac positions can be found from page 35 onwards, so that once you know what your Moon Sign is, you can see what part this plays in the overall build-up of your personal character.

If you follow the instructions on the next page you will soon be able to work out exactly what zodiac sign the Moon occupied on the day that you were born and you can then go on to compare the reading for this position with those of your Sun sign and your Ascendant. It is partly the comparison between these three important positions that goes towards making you the unique individual you are.

HOW TO DISCOVER YOUR MOON SIGN

This is a three-stage process. You may need a pen and a piece of paper but if you follow the instructions below the process should only take a minute or so.

STAGE 1 First of all you need to know the Moon Age at the time of your birth. If you look at Moon Table 1, on page 33, you will find all the years between 1919 and 2017 down the left side. Find the year of your birth and then trace across to the right to the month of your birth. Where the two intersect you will find a number. This is the date of the New Moon in the month that you were born. You now need to count forward the number of days between the New Moon and your own birthday. For example, if the New Moon in the month of your birth was shown as being the 6th and you were born on the 20th, your Moon Age Day would be 14. If the New Moon in the month of your birth came after your birthday, you need to count forward from the New Moon in the previous month. If you were born in a Leap Year, remember to count the 29th February. You can tell if your birth year was a Leap Year if the last two digits can be divided by four. Whatever the result, jot this number down so that you do not forget it.

STAGE 2 Take a look at Moon Table 2 on page 34. Down the left hand column look for the date of your birth. Now trace across to the month of your birth. Where the two meet you will find a letter. Copy this letter down alongside your Moon Age Day.

STAGE 3 Moon Table 3 on page 34 will supply you with the zodiac sign the Moon occupied on the day of your birth. Look for your Moon Age Day down the left hand column and then for the letter you found in Stage 2. Where the two converge you will find a zodiac sign and this is the sign occupied by the Moon on the day that you were born.

Your Zodiac Moon Sign Explained

You will find a profile of all zodiac Moon Signs on pages 35 to 38, showing in yet another way how astrology helps to make you into the individual that you are. In each daily entry of the Astral Diary you can find the zodiac position of the Moon for every day of the year. This also allows you to discover your lunar birthdays. Since the Moon passes through all the signs of the zodiac in about a month, you can expect something like twelve lunar birthdays each year. At these times you are likely to be emotionally steady and able to make the sort of decisions that have real, lasting value.

MOON TABLE 1

YEAR	FEB	MAR	APR	YEAR	FEB	MAR	APR	YEAR	FEB	MAR	APR
1919	–	2/31	30	1952	25	25	24	1985	19	21	20
1920	19	20	18	1953	14	15	13	1986	9	10	9
1921	8	9	8	1954	3	5	3	1987	28	29	28
1922	26	28	27	1955	22	24	22	1988	17	18	16
1923	15	17	16	1956	11	12	11	1989	6	7	6
1924	5	5	4	1957	–	1/31	29	1990	25	26	25
1925	23	24	23	1958	18	20	19	1991	14	15	13
1926	12	14	12	1959	7	9	8	1992	3	4	3
1927	2	3	2	1960	26	27	26	1993	22	24	22
1928	19	21	20	1961	15	16	15	1994	10	12	11
1929	9	11	9	1962	5	6	5	1995	29	30	29
1930	28	30	28	1963	23	25	23	1996	18	19	18
1931	17	19	18	1964	13	14	12	1997	7	9	7
1932	6	7	6	1965	1	2	1	1998	26	27	26
1933	24	26	24	1966	19	21	20	1999	16	17	16
1934	14	15	13	1967	9	10	9	2000	5	6	4
1935	3	5	3	1968	28	29	28	2001	23	24	23
1936	22	23	21	1969	17	18	16	2002	12	13	12
1937	11	13	12	1970	6	7	6	2003	–	2	1
1938	–	2/31	30	1971	25	26	25	2004	20	21	19
1939	19	20	19	1972	14	15	13	2005	9	10	8
1940	8	9	7	1973	4	5	3	2006	28	29	27
1941	26	27	26	1974	22	24	22	2007	15	18	17
1942	15	16	15	1975	11	12	11	2008	6	7	6
1943	4	6	4	1976	29	30	29	2009	25	26	25
1944	24	24	22	1977	18	19	18	2010	14	15	14
1945	12	14	12	1978	7	9	7	2011	3	5	3
1946	2	3	2	1979	26	27	26	2012	22	22	21
1947	19	21	20	1980	15	16	15	2013	10	12	10
1948	9	11	9	1981	4	6	4	2014	1	1/31	30
1949	27	29	28	1982	23	24	23	2015	19	20	19
1950	16	18	17	1983	13	14	13	2016	8	8	7
1951	6	7	6	1984	1	2	1	2017	25	27	25

TABLE 2   MOON TABLE 3

DAY	MAR	APR	M/D	F	G	H	I	J	K	L
1	F	J	0	PI	PI	AR	AR	AR	TA	TA
2	G	J	1	PI	AR	AR	AR	TA	TA	TA
3	G	J	2	AR	AR	AR	TA	TA	TA	GE
4	G	J	3	AR	AR	TA	TA	TA	GE	GE
5	G	J	4	AR	TA	TA	GE	GE	GE	GE
6	G	J	5	TA	TA	GE	GE	GE	CA	CA
7	G	J	6	TA	GE	GE	GE	CA	CA	CA
8	G	J	7	GE	GE	GE	CA	CA	CA	LE
9	G	J	8	GE	GE	CA	CA	CA	LE	LE
10	G	J	9	CA	CA	CA	CA	LE	LE	VI
11	G	K	10	CA	CA	LE	LE	LE	VI	VI
12	H	K	11	CA	LE	LE	LE	VI	VI	VI
13	H	K	12	LE	LE	LE	VI	VI	VI	LI
14	H	K	13	LE	LE	VI	VI	VI	LI	LI
15	H	K	14	VI	VI	VI	LI	LI	LI	LI
16	H	K	15	VI	VI	LI	LI	LI	SC	SC
17	H	K	16	VI	LI	LI	LI	SC	SC	SC
18	H	K	17	LI	LI	LI	SC	SC	SC	SA
19	H	K	18	LI	LI	SC	SC	SC	SA	SA
20	H	K	19	LI	SC	SC	SC	SA	SA	SA
21	H	L	20	SC	SC	SA	SA	SA	CP	CP
22	I	L	21	SC	SA	SA	SA	CP	CP	CP
23	I	L	22	SC	SA	SA	CP	CP	CP	AQ
24	I	L	23	SA	SA	CP	CP	CP	AQ	AQ
25	I	L	24	SA	CP	CP	CP	AQ	AQ	AQ
26	I	L	25	CP	CP	AQ	AQ	AQ	PI	PI
27	I	L	26	CP	AQ	AQ	AQ	PI	PI	PI
28	I	L	27	AQ	AQ	AQ	PI	PI	PI	AR
29	I	L	28	AQ	AQ	PI	PI	PI	AR	AR
30	I	L	29	AQ	PI	PI	PI	AR	AR	AR
31	I	–								

AR = Aries, TA = Taurus, GE = Gemini, CA = Cancer, LE = Leo, VI = Virgo,
LI = Libra, SC = Scorpio, SA = Sagittarius, CP = Capricorn, AQ = Aquarius, PI = Pisces

MOON SIGNS

Moon in Aries

You have a strong imagination, courage, determination and a desire to do things in your own way and forge your own path through life.

Originality is a key attribute; you are seldom stuck for ideas although your mind is changeable and you could take the time to focus on individual tasks. Often quick-tempered, you take orders from few people and live life at a fast pace. Avoid health problems by taking regular time out for rest and relaxation.

Emotionally, it is important that you talk to those you are closest to and work out your true feelings. Once you discover that people are there to help, there is less necessity for you to do everything yourself.

Moon in Taurus

The Moon in Taurus gives you a courteous and friendly manner, which means you are likely to have many friends.

The good things in life mean a lot to you, as Taurus is an Earth sign that delights in experiences which please the senses. Hence you are probably a lover of good food and drink, which may in turn mean you need to keep an eye on the bathroom scales, especially as looking good is also important to you.

Emotionally you are fairly stable and you stick by your own standards. Taureans do not respond well to change. Intuition also plays an important part in your life.

Moon in Gemini

You have a warm-hearted character, sympathetic and eager to help others. At times reserved, you can also be articulate and chatty: this is part of the paradox of Gemini, which always brings duplicity to the nature. You are interested in current affairs, have a good intellect, and are good company and likely to have many friends. Most of your friends have a high opinion of you and would be ready to defend you should the need arise. However, this is usually unnecessary, as you are quite capable of defending yourself in any verbal confrontation.

Travel is important to your inquisitive mind and you find intellectual stimulus in mixing with people from different cultures. You also gain much from reading, writing and the arts but you do need plenty of rest and relaxation in order to avoid fatigue.

Moon in Cancer

The Moon in Cancer at the time of birth is a fortunate position as Cancer is the Moon's natural home. This means that the qualities of compassion and understanding given by the Moon are especially enhanced in your nature, and you are friendly and sociable and cope well with emotional pressures. You cherish home and family life, and happily do the domestic tasks. Your surroundings are important to you and you hate squalor and filth. You are likely to have a love of music and poetry.

Your basic character, although at times changeable like the Moon itself, depends on symmetry. You aim to make your surroundings comfortable and harmonious, for yourself and those close to you.

Moon in Leo

The best qualities of the Moon and Leo come together to make you warm-hearted, fair, ambitious and self-confident. With good organisational abilities, you invariably rise to a position of responsibility in your chosen career. This is fortunate as you don't enjoy being an 'also-ran' and would rather be an important part of a small organisation than a menial in a large one.

You should be lucky in love, and happy, provided you put in the effort to make a comfortable home for yourself and those close to you. It is likely that you will have a love of pleasure, sport, music and literature. Life brings you many rewards, most of them as a direct result of your own efforts, although you may be luckier than average and ready to make the best of any situation.

Moon in Virgo

You are endowed with good mental abilities and a keen receptive memory, but you are never ostentatious or pretentious. Naturally quite reserved, you still have many friends, especially of the opposite sex. Marital relationships must be discussed carefully and worked at so that they remain harmonious, as personal attachments can be a problem if you do not give them your full attention.

Talented and persevering, you possess artistic qualities and are a good homemaker. Earning your honours through genuine merit, you work long and hard towards your objectives but show little pride in your achievements. Many short journeys will be undertaken in your life.

Moon in Libra

With the Moon in Libra you are naturally popular and make friends easily. People like you, probably more than you realise, you bring fun to a party and are a natural diplomat. For all its good points, Libra is not the most stable of astrological signs and, as a result, your emotions can be a little unstable too. Therefore, although the Moon in Libra is said to be good for love and marriage, your Sun sign and Rising sign will have an important effect on your emotional and loving qualities.

You must remember to relate to others in your decision-making. Co-operation is crucial because Libra represents the 'balance' of life that can only be achieved through harmonious relationships. Conformity is not easy for you because Libra, an Air sign, likes its independence.

Moon in Scorpio

Some people might call you pushy. In fact, all you really want to do is to live life to the full and protect yourself and your family from the pressures of life. Take care to avoid giving the impression of being sarcastic or impulsive and use your energies wisely and constructively.

You have great courage and you invariably achieve your goals by force of personality and sheer effort. You are fond of mystery and are good at predicting the outcome of situations and events. Travel experiences can be beneficial to you.

You may experience problems if you do not take time to examine your motives in a relationship, and also if you allow jealousy, always a feature of Scorpio, to cloud your judgement.

Moon in Sagittarius

The Moon in Sagittarius helps to make you a generous individual with humanitarian qualities and a kind heart. Restlessness may be intrinsic as your mind is seldom still. Perhaps because of this, you have a need for change that could lead you to several major moves during your adult life. You are not afraid to stand your ground when you know your judgement is right, you speak directly and have good intuition.

At work you are quick, efficient and versatile and so you make an ideal employee. You need work to be intellectually demanding and do not enjoy tedious routines.

In relationships, you anger quickly if faced with stupidity or deception, though you are just as quick to forgive and forget. Emotionally, there are times when your heart rules your head.

Moon in Capricorn

The Moon in Capricorn makes you popular and likely to come into the public eye in some way. The watery Moon is not entirely comfortable in the Earth sign of Capricorn and this may lead to some difficulties in the early years of life. An initial lack of creative ability and indecision must be overcome before the true qualities of patience and perseverance inherent in Capricorn can show through.

You have good administrative ability and are a capable worker, and if you are careful you can accumulate wealth. But you must be cautious and take professional advice in partnerships, as you are open to deception. You may be interested in social or welfare work, which suit your organisational skills and sympathy for others.

Moon in Aquarius

The Moon in Aquarius makes you an active and agreeable person with a friendly, easy-going nature. Sympathetic to the needs of others, you flourish in a laid-back atmosphere. You are broad-minded, fair and open to suggestion, although sometimes you have an unconventional quality which others can find hard to understand.

You are interested in the strange and curious, and in old articles and places. You enjoy trips to these places and gain much from them. Political, scientific and educational work interests you and you might choose a career in science or technology.

Money-wise, you make gains through innovation and concentration and Lunar Aquarians often tackle more than one job at a time. In love you are kind and honest.

Moon in Pisces

You have a kind, sympathetic nature, somewhat retiring at times, but you always take account of others' feelings and help when you can.

Personal relationships may be problematic, but as life goes on you can learn from your experiences and develop a better understanding of yourself and the world around you.

You have a fondness for travel, appreciate beauty and harmony and hate disorder and strife. You may be fond of literature and would make a good writer or speaker yourself. You have a creative imagination and may come across as an incurable romantic. You have strong intuition, maybe bordering on a mediumistic quality, which sets you apart from the mass. You may not be rich in cash terms, but your personal gifts are worth more than gold.

ARIES IN LOVE

Discover how compatible in love you are with people from the same and other signs of the zodiac. Five stars equals a match made in heaven!

Aries meets Aries

This could be an all-or-nothing pairing. Both parties are from a dominant sign, so someone will have to be flexible in order to maintain personal harmony. Both know what they want out of life, and may have trouble overcoming any obstacles a relationship creates. This is a good physical pairing, with a chemistry that few other matches enjoy to the same level. Attitude is everything, but at least there is a mutual admiration that makes gazing at your partner like looking in the mirror. Star rating: ****

Aries meets Taurus

This is a match that has been known to work very well. Aries brings dynamism and ambition, while Taurus has the patience to see things through logically. Such complementary views work equally well in a relationship or in the office. There is mutual respect, but sometimes a lack of total understanding. The romantic needs of each are quite different, but both are still fulfilled. They can live easily in domestic harmony which is very important but, interestingly, Aries may be the loser in battles of will. Star rating: ***

Aries meets Gemini

Don't expect peace and harmony with this combination, although what comes along instead might make up for any disagreements. Gemini has a very fertile imagination, while Aries has the tenacity to make reality from fantasy. Combined, they have a sizzling relationship. There are times when both parties could explode with indignation and something has to give. But even if there are clashes, making them up will always be most enjoyable! Mutual financial success is likely in this match. Star rating: ****

Aries meets Cancer

A potentially one-sided pairing, it often appears that the Cancerian is brow-beaten by the far more dominant Arian. So much depends on the patience of the Cancerian individual, because if good psychology is present – who knows? But beware, Aries, you may find your partner too passive, and constantly having to take the lead can be wearing – even for you. A prolonged trial period would be advantageous, as the match could easily go either way. When it does work, though, this relationship is usually contented. Star rating: ***

Aries meets Leo

Stand by for action and make sure the house is sound-proof. Leo is a lofty idealist and there is always likely to be friction when two Fire signs meet. To compensate, there is much mutual admiration, together with a desire to please. Where there are shared incentives, the prognosis is good but it's important not to let little irritations blow up. Both signs want to have their own way and this is a sure cause of trouble. There might not be much patience here, but there is plenty of action. Star rating: *****

Aries meets Virgo

Neither of these signs really understands the other, and that could easily lead to a clash. Virgo is so pedantic, which will drive Aries up the wall, while Aries always wants to be moving on to the next objective, before Virgo is even settled with the last one. It will take time for these two to get to know each other, but this is a great business matching. If a personal relationship is seen in these terms then the prognosis can be good, but on the whole, this is not an inspiring match. Star rating: ***

Aries meets Libra

These signs are zodiac opposites which means a make-or-break situation. The match will either be a great success or a dismal failure. Why? Well Aries finds it difficult to understand the flighty Air-sign tendencies of Libra, whilst the natural balance of Libra contradicts the unorthodox Arian methods. Any flexibility will come from Libra, which may mean that things work out for a while, but Libra only has so much patience and it may eventually run out. In the end, Aries may be just too bossy for an independent but sensitive sign like Libra. Star rating: **

Aries meets Scorpio

There can be great affection here, even if the two zodiac signs are so very different. The common link is the planet Mars, which plays a part in both these natures. Although Aries is, outwardly, the most dominant, Scorpio people are among the most powerful to be found anywhere. This quiet determination is respected by Aries. Aries will satisfy the passionate side of Scorpio, particularly with instruction from Scorpio. There are mysteries here which will add spice to life. The few arguments that do occur are likely to be awe-inspiring. Star rating: ****

Aries meets Sagittarius

This can be one of the most favourable matches of them all. Both Aries and Sagittarius are Fire signs, which often leads to clashes of will, but this pair find a mutual understanding. Sagittarius helps Aries to develop a better sense of humour, while Aries teaches the Archer about consistency on the road to success. Some patience is called for on both sides, but these people have a natural liking for each other. Add this to growing love and you have a long-lasting combination that is hard to beat. Star rating: *****

Aries meets Capricorn

Capricorn works conscientiously to achieve its objectives and so can be the perfect companion for Aries. The Ram knows how to achieve but not how to consolidate, so the two signs have a great deal to offer one another practically. There may not be fireworks and it's sometimes doubtful how well they know each other, but it may not matter. Aries is outwardly hot but inwardly cool, whilst Capricorn can appear low key but be a furnace underneath. Such a pairing can gradually find contentment, though both parties may wonder how this is so. Star rating: ****

Aries meets Aquarius

Aquarius is an Air sign, and Air and Fire often work well together, but perhaps not in the case of Aries and Aquarius. The average Aquarian lives in what the Ram sees as a fantasy world, so without a sufficiently good meeting of minds, compromise may be lacking. Of course, almost anything is possible, and the dominant side of Aries could be trained by the devil-may-care attitude of Aquarius. There are meeting points but they are difficult to establish. However, given sufficient time and an open mind on both sides, a degree of happiness is possible. Star rating: **

Aries meets Pisces

Still waters run deep, and they don't come much deeper than Pisces. Although these signs share the same quadrant of the zodiac, they have little in common. Pisces is a dreamer, a romantic idealist with steady and spiritual goals. Aries needs to be on the move, and has very different ideals. It's hard to see how a relationship could develop because the outlook on life is so different but, with patience, especially from Aries, there is a chance that things might work out. Pisces needs incentive, and Aries may be the sign to offer it. Star rating: **

VENUS:
THE PLANET OF LOVE

If you look up at the sky around sunset or sunrise you will often see Venus in close attendance to the Sun. It is arguably one of the most beautiful sights of all and there is little wonder that historically it became associated with the goddess of love. But although Venus does play an important part in the way you view love and in the way others see you romantically, this is only one of the spheres of influence that it enjoys in your overall character.

Venus has a part to play in the more cultured side of your life and has much to do with your appreciation of art, literature, music and general creativity. Even the way you look is responsive to the part of the zodiac that Venus occupied at the start of your life, though this fact is also down to your Sun sign and Ascending sign. If, at the time you were born, Venus occupied one of the more gregarious zodiac signs, you will be more likely to wear your heart on your sleeve, as well as to be more attracted to entertainment, social gatherings and good company. If on the other hand Venus occupied a quiet zodiac sign at the time of your birth, you would tend to be more retiring and less willing to shine in public situations.

It's good to know what part the planet Venus plays in your life for it can have a great bearing on the way you appear to the rest of the world and since we all have to mix with others, you can learn to make the very best of what Venus has to offer you.

One of the great complications in the past has always been trying to establish exactly what zodiac position Venus enjoyed when you were born because the planet is notoriously difficult to track. However, we have solved that problem by creating a table that is exclusive to your Sun sign, which you will find on the following page.

Establishing your Venus sign could not be easier. Just look up the year of your birth on the following page and you will see a sign of the zodiac. This was the sign that Venus occupied in the period covered by your sign in that year. If Venus occupied more than one sign during the period, this is indicated by the date on which the sign changed, and the name of the new sign. For instance, if you were born in 1950, Venus was in Aquarius until the 7th April, after which time it was in Pisces. If you were born before 7th April your Venus sign is Aquarius, if you were born on or after 7th April, your Venus sign is Pisces. Once you have established the position of Venus at the time of your birth, you can then look in the pages which follow to see how this has a bearing on your life as a whole.

1919 ARIES / 24.3 TAURUS
1920 PISCES / 14.4 ARIES
1921 TAURUS
1922 ARIES / 13.4 TAURUS
1923 AQUARIUS / 1.4 PISCES
1924 TAURUS / 6.4 GEMINI
1925 PISCES / 28.3 ARIES
1926 AQUARIUS / 6.4 PISCES
1927 ARIES / 24.3 TAURUS
1928 PISCES / 13.4 ARIES
1929 TAURUS / 20.4 ARIES
1930 ARIES / 13.4 TAURUS
1931 AQUARIUS / 31.3 PISCES
1932 TAURUS / 6.4 GEMINI
1933 PISCES / 27.3 ARIES
1934 AQUARIUS / 6.4 PISCES
1935 ARIES / 23.3 TAURUS
1936 PISCES / 13.4 ARIES
1937 TAURUS / 14.4 ARIES
1938 ARIES / 12.4 TAURUS
1939 AQUARIUS / 31.3 PISCES
1940 TAURUS / 5.4 GEMINI
1941 PISCES / 26.3 ARIES /
    20.4 TAURUS
1942 AQUARIUS / 7.4 PISCES
1943 ARIES / 23.3 TAURUS
1944 PISCES / 12.4 ARIES
1945 TAURUS / 8.4 ARIES
1946 ARIES / 12.4 TAURUS
1947 AQUARIUS / 30.3 PISCES
1948 TAURUS / 5.4 GEMINI
1949 PISCES / 25.3 ARIES /
    20.4 TAURUS
1950 AQUARIUS / 7.4 PISCES
1951 ARIES / 22.3 TAURUS
1952 PISCES / 12.4 ARIES
1953 TAURUS / 1.4 ARIES
1954 ARIES / 11.4 TAURUS
1955 AQUARIUS / 30.3 PISCES
1956 TAURUS / 4.4 GEMINI
1957 PISCES / 25.3 ARIES /
    19.4 TAURUS
1958 AQUARIUS / 8.4 PISCES
1959 ARIES / 22.3 TAURUS
1960 PISCES / 11.4 ARIES
1961 ARIES
1962 ARIES / 11.4 TAURUS
1963 AQUARIUS / 29.3 PISCES
1964 TAURUS / 4.4 GEMINI
1965 ARIES / 24.3 ARIES /
    19.4 TAURUS
1966 AQUARIUS / 8.4 PISCES
1967 TAURUS / 20.4 GEMINI
1968 PISCES / 10.4 ARIES

1969 ARIES
1970 ARIES / 10.4 TAURUS
1971 AQUARIUS / 29.3 PISCES
1972 TAURUS / 3.4 GEMINI
1973 PISCES / 24.3 ARIES /
    18.4 TAURUS
1974 AQUARIUS / 8.4 PISCES
1975 TAURUS / 19.4 GEMINI
1976 PISCES / 10.4 ARIES
1977 ARIES
1978 ARIES / 10.4 TAURUS
1979 AQUARIUS / 28.3 PISCES
1980 TAURUS / 3.4 GEMINI
1981 PISCES / 23.3 ARIES /
    18.4 TAURUS
1982 AQUARIUS / 9.4 PISCES
1983 TAURUS / 19.4 GEMINI
1984 PISCES / 9.4 ARIES
1985 ARIES
1986 ARIES / 9.4 TAURUS
1987 AQUARIUS / 28.3 PISCES
1988 TAURUS / 2.4 GEMINI
1989 PISCES / 23.3 ARIES /
    17.4 TAURUS
1990 AQUARIUS / 9.4 PISCES
1991 TAURUS / 18.4 GEMINI
1992 PISCES / 9.4 ARIES
1993 ARIES
1994 ARIES / 9.4 TAURUS
1995 AQUARIUS / 27.3 PISCES
1996 TAURUS / 2.4 GEMINI
1997 PISCES / 22.3 ARIES /
    17.4 TAURUS
1998 AQUARIUS / 9.4 PISCES
1999 TAURUS / 18.4 GEMINI
2000 PISCES / 9.4 ARIES
2001 ARIES
2002 ARIES / 7.4 TAURUS
2003 AQUARIUS / 27.3 PISCES
2004 TAURUS / 1.4 GEMINI
2005 PISCES/22.3 ARIES
2006 AQUARIUS/7.4 PISCES
2007 TAURUS / 16.4 GEMINI
2008 PISCES / 9.4 ARIES
2009 ARIES
2010 ARIES / 7.4 TAURUS
2011 AQUARIUS / 27.3 PISCES
2012 TAURUS / 1.4 GEMINI
2013 PISCES / 22.3 ARIES
2014 AQUARIUS / 7.4 PISCES
2015 TAURUS / 16.4 GEMINI
2016 PISCES / 9.4 ARIES
2017 TAURUS / 1.4 GEMINI

44

VENUS THROUGH
THE ZODIAC SIGNS

Venus in Aries

Amongst other things, the position of Venus in Aries indicates a fondness for travel, music and all creative pursuits. Your nature tends to be affectionate and you would try not to create confusion or difficulty for others if it could be avoided. Many people with this planetary position have a great love of the theatre, and mental stimulation is of the greatest importance. Early romantic attachments are common with Venus in Aries, so it is very important to establish a genuine sense of romantic continuity. Early marriage is not recommended, especially if it is based on sympathy. You may give your heart a little too readily on occasions.

Venus in Taurus

You are capable of very deep feelings and your emotions tend to last for a very long time. This makes you a trusting partner and lover, whose constancy is second to none. In life you are precise and careful and always try to do things the right way. Although this means an ordered life, which you are comfortable with, it can also lead you to be rather too fussy for your own good. Despite your pleasant nature, you are very fixed in your opinions and quite able to speak your mind. Others are attracted to you and historical astrologers always quoted this position of Venus as being very fortunate in terms of marriage. However, if you find yourself involved in a failed relationship, it could take you a long time to trust again.

Venus in Gemini

As with all associations related to Gemini, you tend to be quite versatile, anxious for change and intelligent in your dealings with the world at large. You may gain money from more than one source but you are equally good at spending it. There is an inference here that you are a good communicator, via either the written or the spoken word, and you love to be in the company of interesting people. Always on the look-out for culture, you may also be very fond of music, and love to indulge the curious and cultured side of your nature. In romance you tend to have more than one relationship and could find yourself associated with someone who has previously been a friend or even a distant relative.

Venus in Cancer

You often stay close to home because you are very fond of family and enjoy many of your most treasured moments when you are with those you love. Being naturally sympathetic, you will always do anything you can to support those around you, even people you hardly know at all. This charitable side of your nature is your most noticeable trait and is one of the reasons why others are naturally so fond of you. Being receptive and in some cases even psychic, you can see through to the soul of most of those with whom you come into contact. You may not commence too many romantic attachments but when you do give your heart, it tends to be unconditionally.

Venus in Leo

It must become quickly obvious to almost anyone you meet that you are kind, sympathetic and yet determined enough to stand up for anyone or anything that is truly important to you. Bright and sunny, you warm the world with your natural enthusiasm and would rarely do anything to hurt those around you, or at least not intentionally. In romance you are ardent and sincere, though some may find your style just a little overpowering. Gains come through your contacts with other people and this could be especially true with regard to romance, for love and money often come hand in hand for those who were born with Venus in Leo. People claim to understand you, though you are more complex than you seem.

Venus in Virgo

Your nature could well be fairly quiet no matter what your Sun sign might be, though this fact often manifests itself as an inner peace and would not prevent you from being basically sociable. Some delays and even the odd disappointment in love cannot be ruled out with this planetary position, though it's a fact that you will usually find the happiness you look for in the end. Catapulting yourself into romantic entanglements that you know to be rather ill-advised is not sensible, and it would be better to wait before you committed yourself exclusively to any one person. It is the essence of your nature to serve the world at large and through doing so it is possible that you will attract money at some stage in your life.

Venus in Libra

Venus is very comfortable in Libra and bestows upon those people who have this planetary position a particular sort of kindness that is easy to recognise. This is a very good position for all sorts of friendships and also for romantic attachments that usually bring much joy into your life. Few individuals with Venus in Libra would avoid marriage and since you are capable of great depths of love, it is likely that you will find a contented personal life. You like to mix with people of integrity and intelligence but don't take kindly to scruffy surroundings or work that means getting your hands too dirty. Careful speculation, good business dealings and money through marriage all seem fairly likely.

Venus in Scorpio

You are quite open and tend to spend money quite freely, even on those occasions when you don't have very much. Although your intentions are always good, there are times when you get yourself in to the odd scrape and this can be particularly true when it comes to romance, which you may come to late or from a rather unexpected direction. Certainly you have the power to be happy and to make others contented on the way, but you find the odd stumbling block on your journey through life and it could seem that you have to work harder than those around you. As a result of this, you gain a much deeper understanding of the true value of personal happiness than many people ever do, and are likely to achieve true contentment in the end.

Venus in Sagittarius

You are lighthearted, cheerful and always able to see the funny side of any situation. These facts enhance your popularity, which is especially high with members of the opposite sex. You should never have to look too far to find romantic interest in your life, though it is just possible that you might be too willing to commit yourself before you are certain that the person in question is right for you. Part of the problem here extends to other areas of life too. The fact is that you like variety in everything and so can tire of situations that fail to offer it. All the same, if you choose wisely and learn to understand your restless side, then great happiness can be yours.

Venus in Capricorn

The most notable trait that comes from Venus in this position is that it makes you trustworthy and able to take on all sorts of responsibilities in life. People are instinctively fond of you and love you all the more because you are always ready to help those who are in any form of need. Social and business popularity can be yours and there is a magnetic quality to your nature that is particularly attractive in a romantic sense. Anyone who wants a partner for a lover, a spouse and a good friend too would almost certainly look in your direction. Constancy is the hallmark of your nature and unfaithfulness would go right against the grain. You might sometimes be a little too trusting.

Venus in Aquarius

This location of Venus offers a fondness for travel and a desire to try out something new at every possible opportunity. You are extremely easy to get along with and tend to have many friends from varied backgrounds, classes and inclinations. You like to live a distinct sort of life and gain a great deal from moving about, both in a career sense and with regard to your home. It is not out of the question that you could form a romantic attachment to someone who comes from far away or be attracted to a person of a distinctly artistic and original nature. What you cannot stand is jealousy, for you have friends of both sexes and would want to keep things that way.

Venus in Pisces

The first thing people tend to notice about you is your wonderful, warm smile. Being very charitable by nature you will do anything to help others, even if you don't know them well. Much of your life may be spent sorting out situations for other people, but it is very important to feel that you are living for yourself too. In the main, you remain cheerful, and tend to be quite attractive to members of the opposite sex. Where romantic attachments are concerned, you could be drawn to people who are significantly older or younger than yourself or to someone with a unique career or point of view. It might be best for you to avoid marrying whilst you are still very young.

ARIES:
2016 DIARY PAGES

October

2016

1 SATURDAY
Moon Age Day 1   Moon Sign Libra

Certain expectations will probably have to be played down today. Although the lunar low doesn't have too much of a bearing on your life you could be feeling as though things are not turning out entirely as you would wish. Take advantage of good social possibilities towards the end of the day

2 SUNDAY
Moon Age Day 2   Moon Sign Libra

Although there is little in the way of self-discipline about at this time, perhaps you should tell yourself that this is, after all, a Sunday. You are entitled to some time away from responsibility and should not get irritated with yourself simply because you do not feel like putting yourself out for purely practical reasons.

3 MONDAY
Moon Age Day 3   Moon Sign Scorpio

There may be certain issues to bear in mind when you are dealing with others today and a sympathetic attitude would clearly work best. It is possible that in one way or another you could be feeling put upon, though in reality all you need to do is to talk things through to find even usually difficult people easy to handle.

4 TUESDAY
Moon Age Day 4   Moon Sign Scorpio

This is one of the best days of the month for being in social situations and for getting on well with people generally. Some of the more critical types who were around earlier in the month are now less in evidence. Make the most of outings or the chance to meet new people on a one-to-one basis.

5 WEDNESDAY *Moon Age Day 5 Moon Sign Scorpio*

It is possible that for the first time in many days you will find at least some people unresponsive and difficult to deal with. This is a sign that you need to concentrate your efforts more specifically. Routines could get on your nerves for a few days but it will still be necessary to sort out some important details.

6 THURSDAY *Moon Age Day 6 Moon Sign Sagittarius*

Along comes a phase that definitely does benefit personal relationships. You should discover now that things do go better in pairs and that you have all you need to get your own way. What won't help is that Aries tendency to dominate either people or situations. An easy-going attitude definitely works best today.

7 FRIDAY *Moon Age Day 7 Moon Sign Sagittarius*

A long-standing commitment needs extra thinking about right now. Rules and regulations should be easier than usual to deal with, perhaps because you tend to make them up for yourself as you go along today. Your means of communication is good and some better luck may show itself later in the day.

8 SATURDAY *Moon Age Day 8 Moon Sign Capricorn*

Today marks the start of a transitional period during which many factors in your life will have to be looked at in a new and perhaps a very different way. A little physical discomfort of some sort almost certainly won't last long, though this may not be the best time for embarking on some new keep fit routine.

9 SUNDAY *Moon Age Day 9 Moon Sign Capricorn*

The social world, though quite clearly busy, may have less to offer you than has been the case for the last week or so. This shouldn't worry you too much. On the contrary you now turn your attention towards more practical issues and can be fairly ruthless when dealing with matters you know to be of supreme importance.

10 MONDAY   *Moon Age Day 10   Moon Sign Capricorn*

There is a strong tendency at the start of this week for you to cast your mind backward, towards specific aspects of the past. Whether or not there is any practical gain to be had from this pursuit remains to be seen. What is clear is that you need to keep at least one eye on the future too.

11 TUESDAY   *Moon Age Day 11   Moon Sign Aquarius*

No matter how you choose to express yourself at the moment there is a definite chance that you will run into some problems. It might be suggested that the best way round this sort of dilemma is to keep your mouth shut altogether, at least for now. These trends don't really have a bearing on personal attachments.

12 WEDNESDAY   *Moon Age Day 12   Moon Sign Aquarius*

Your main concern right now is to improve your life in just about any way you find to be possible. The way forward is towards a greater degree of simplicity and to spend time with tasks that don't demand too much of you. Alterations to the periphery of life can have a great bearing further down the line, too.

13 THURSDAY   *Moon Age Day 13   Moon Sign Pisces*

Look out for an 'off with the old and on with the new' sort of attitude which develops around now. Whatever is not working well in your life should probably be abandoned, in favour of alterations that bring you more in line with the way things should be. Personal attachments remain untouched by these trends.

14 FRIDAY   *Moon Age Day 14   Moon Sign Pisces*

It may be that trying to please too many people today is something of a mistake. Better by far to concentrate your efforts on those you know well. Avoid saying 'yes' simply for the sake of popularity, since this is only likely to bring you some problems further down the line, when you will have to be honest.

15 SATURDAY   *Moon Age Day 15   Moon Sign Aries*

The Moon moves into your sign and should bring with it a number of opportunities that look especially good. This is not a time when you will want to spend hours sorting out details. Once you have made up your mind to a specific course of action, get stuck in and show the world what you are made of.

16 SUNDAY   *Moon Age Day 16   Moon Sign Aries*

This is almost certainly not a day to be too careful. The odd gamble can pay off well, as long as you make sure that you do not ignore your intuition, which works well right now. Financial objectives in particular are dealt with easily but you have an especially good ability to get on with those around you.

17 MONDAY   *Moon Age Day 17   Moon Sign Taurus*

All aspects of communication are lively at this time. With some entertaining people on the horizon and almost everything going your way, the time has come to put your thoughts into tangible form. Almost anyone will be pleased to hear what you have to say and their reactions could be surprising.

18 TUESDAY   *Moon Age Day 18   Moon Sign Taurus*

You will now be at your most contented when you are on the move. Try to avoid staying too long in one place and keep your interests light and perhaps even superficial. What you definitely don't want at present is to be bogged down by circumstances and situations that you find boring.

19 WEDNESDAY   *Moon Age Day 19   Moon Sign Gemini*

Your daily life is likely to be busier than ever, with material considerations taking the centre stage position. Get a few jobs out of the way today, even though they are not strictly necessary at this time. Later in the week your schedule is likely to be very rushed and you will need all the spare moments you can find.

20 THURSDAY   *Moon Age Day 20   Moon Sign Gemini*

Where social matters are concerned you seem to be on top form. Mixing and mingling with a whole host of different types, you have the bit between your teeth when it comes to organising events and get-togethers. Romance is close for some Aries types, especially the young or young-at-heart.

21 FRIDAY   *Moon Age Day 21   Moon Sign Cancer*

Most fulfilment today will come from private and domestic matters. It won't be possible for you to remove yourself from the real world altogether, but that is what you may feel like doing at times. This sort of Aries is rarely seen and your general attitude could prove to be quite a mystery to some.

22 SATURDAY   *Moon Age Day 22   Moon Sign Cancer*

The emphasis is on material security and you are still unlikely to be biting off as much as you often do. Now you are steadier in your thought processes and more willing to see tasks through to their logical end. Socially speaking you are happy and sunny – in fact the perfect Aries as far as most people are concerned.

23 SUNDAY   *Moon Age Day 23   Moon Sign Leo*

A high profile can be all-important today. The Moon is in Leo and so is angled well to your Sun sign. Other planetary indications assure you of a greater degree of popularity and an ability to get on side with people who might not have given you reason to believe they were particularly keen on you before.

24 MONDAY   *Moon Age Day 24   Moon Sign Leo*

Your most meaningful moments today are with family members and friends who have been a part of your life for a long time. This would be a good day for domestic shopping or for making some sort of change around the house; possibly one that is geared towards your comfort in the winter months ahead.

25 TUESDAY
Moon Age Day 25   Moon Sign Leo

Your social popularity is still very high. Splitting your time between friends and those at home is something you will have to try hard to achieve right now. It isn't always going to be easy but then taking the simple path in life isn't of that much interest to the average Aries individual.

26 WEDNESDAY
Moon Age Day 26   Moon Sign Virgo

If you find yourself at loggerheads regarding a joint financial matter it would be best to stand back and try to look at things from a totally impartial point of view. Avoid getting tied up in red tape because your natural reaction at the moment would be to push your way through it. That could make you some enemies.

27 THURSDAY
Moon Age Day 27   Moon Sign Virgo

You now tend to back down in discussions at home, whilst out there in the wider world you stick up for yourself totally. If you work with someone you love the result might be rather confusing. This duality of nature is not typical of your zodiac sign at all, so thank goodness it is a very temporary phenomenon.

28 FRIDAY
Moon Age Day 28   Moon Sign Libra

This is generally a good time to play life steadily and not to attempt any major coup, particularly in a business sense. Once you have decided on a particular course of action you might have to wait until after the weekend to put it into action. In extreme cases it will be a few days before you can make genuine progress.

29 SATURDAY
Moon Age Day 29   Moon Sign Libra

If there are genuine setbacks now on the road to success, the best way forward is to simply wait and see. With the weekend here it is possible that you have already written off today in terms of practical gains, leaving the field free for personal enjoyment, which is not hindered by present trends.

30 SUNDAY   *Moon Age Day 0   Moon Sign Libra*

Talks with others could prove enlightening during this weekend period. This is likely to be especially true if you are at work, with the possibility of promotion coming along for some Aries people at this time. Keep your most entertaining side hidden until the evening though because there are happy times on offer.

31 MONDAY   *Moon Age Day 1   Moon Sign Scorpio*

You may feel that getting through to others is not half as easy as you would wish today. This said, some of the problems could actually be caused by those other people. The Aries ego isn't burning quite as brightly as usual at present, but don't allow this trend to make you feel that problems are always your fault.

November
2016

1 TUESDAY
Moon Age Day 2   Moon Sign Scorpio

It could be that for some Aries subjects there are slight difficulties surrounding an intimate relationship. Getting this sorted out will be your number one priority. Meanwhile you are also busy in a practical sense and more than willing to share some of your present professional knowledge with others.

2 WEDNESDAY
Moon Age Day 3   Moon Sign Sagittarius

Your idealism is very strong and there isn't much doubt about your determination to follow specific routes, once you have made up your mind. This could make you appear somewhat less than flexible when seen through the eyes of others, a state of affairs that may not help you too much in the short-term.

3 THURSDAY
Moon Age Day 4   Moon Sign Sagittarius

If there is any uncertainty in your life today it can probably be best addressed by turning to someone who is a professional in their own specific field. There are always individuals around who will do everything they can to help you. This is especially true in light of your own willingness to help others.

4 FRIDAY
Moon Age Day 5   Moon Sign Sagittarius

Any chance to strike up some form of new social contract should be grasped with both hands. This is most certainly the case when you are dealing with unconventional types, many of whom seem to be especially attractive to you at this time. Have fun when you are away from work and socialise as much as possible.

5 SATURDAY   *Moon Age Day 6   Moon Sign Capricorn*

The real enjoyment that comes into your life is inclined to do so in and around your home. This has been the tendency for some time now and remains the case across the weekend. You can rely on relatives to do your favours. More importantly, intimate contacts are offering so much more than usual.

6 SUNDAY   *Moon Age Day 7   Moon Sign Capricorn*

The green light is on regarding general progress and you know what you want from life at this time. The true nature of Aries is now beginning to show, offering incentives that have been absent for some time. Grab life with both hands and enjoy the advantages that are now on offer.

7 MONDAY   *Moon Age Day 8   Moon Sign Aquarius*

A light-hearted approach to all matters of love and romance now comes along. With a smile on your face for most of the day you can be an inspiration to others and keep everyone more or less happy. This is the side of Aries that the world really adores and most of the people you meet will share your attitude.

8 TUESDAY   *Moon Age Day 9   Moon Sign Aquarius*

Although you are speaking and acting well at present, it is just possible that some misunderstandings at home could prove to be a problem. You need to find moments to explain yourself fully, even when you are so busy in other ways. Trying to fit in everything you want to do right now won't be easy.

9 WEDNESDAY   *Moon Age Day 10   Moon Sign Pisces*

Social issues have rather less going for them today, which is why it would be sensible to turn your attention towards practicalities instead. At work you are progressive and even dynamic. It won't be long before it seems that the whole world is turning to you for specific advice of the sort that Aries now finds easy to dispense.

10 THURSDAY
Moon Age Day 11   Moon Sign Pisces

A series of pleasurable diversions, away from strictly practical day-to-day issues, are more than likely at this time. Give yourself over fully to having fun when the chance arises and don't be bogged down with details that don't really matter. Creative potential is good, especially in and around your home.

11 FRIDAY
Moon Age Day 12   Moon Sign Pisces

Your home life remains specifically rewarding, though that doesn't mean you are ignoring the more practical aspects of your life. What you manage today is a more than adequate balance, even if it does sometimes appear that you are burning the candle at both ends. Aries resilience is legendary and today you prove it.

12 SATURDAY
Moon Age Day 13   Moon Sign Aries

With the lunar high comes a definite sense of drive and enthusiasm. You shouldn't find it at all hard to ring the changes and you will be much more likely now to spend time away from home. Despite these facts, and the lunar high, you may feel happier if someone you know well is close at hand.

13 SUNDAY
Moon Age Day 14   Moon Sign Aries

Pushing ahead and getting what you want from life are simply two of your talents right now. Energy is returning and you may look back at the last week or so, puzzled at the way you may have behaved. That doesn't matter. Simply strike while the iron is hot. Make gains and have fun, even though this is a Sunday.

14 MONDAY
Moon Age Day 15   Moon Sign Taurus

There are ups and downs to deal with, and fortunately your ability to go to the heart of any specific matter is enhanced now. Gradually you see life as a more positive experience than might have been the case for a few days. Routines are not hard to address. Socially speaking, you may prefer the company of relatives.

15 TUESDAY   *Moon Age Day 16   Moon Sign Taurus*

You need to be very aware of the motives of others at this time, particularly those who may have some sort of interest in fooling you in some way. Keep a high profile when you are in company and don't be put off by the sort of individual who naturally tends to be pessimistic. You can be a guiding force now.

16 WEDNESDAY   *Moon Age Day 17   Moon Sign Gemini*

Don't let emotional issues dominate you today to the point that you forget about the practical matters of life. There are plenty of opportunities for you to make an extremely good impression and the sort of company around that you should find to be both stimulating and of use to you in terms of new ideas.

17 THURSDAY   *Moon Age Day 18   Moon Sign Gemini*

There are changes taking place around you, whether or not you seem to be choosing them for yourself. In those situations where you have no power to alter the state of affairs it's best to go with the flow. Very few situations around you at present would work against your best interests.

18 FRIDAY   *Moon Age Day 19   Moon Sign Cancer*

Today just could seem to be something of a comedown after recent events. Never mind, concentrate instead on the quieter aspects of the day and enjoy the relief of less activity. There should be plenty of people around who would be more than willing to share your leisure hours and who can lift your spirits no end.

19 SATURDAY   *Moon Age Day 20   Moon Sign Cancer*

This continues to be a period of quiet mental stimulus and information. Stay tuned in to all that life is offering and don't allow others to bring you down. Someone you haven't seen for quite some time is likely to turn up again in your life at any time now and may bring some surprises with them.

20 SUNDAY
Moon Age Day 21   Moon Sign Leo

Travel could now be subject to delays, probably through circumstances that are beyond your own control. Stay calm if things do go wrong, or else do what you can to redress the balance. Newer and better powers of communication are coming your way, thanks to changing planetary trends.

21 MONDAY
Moon Age Day 22   Moon Sign Leo

You can clearly enjoy the best of both worlds today. On the one hand life can be romantic and emotionally rewarding, whilst on the other you have the ability to get practical jobs out of the way in no time at all. Your personality is entertaining and it is very easy for others to demonstrate how fond they are of you.

22 TUESDAY
Moon Age Day 23   Moon Sign Virgo

Now is the moment to look at emotional issues in a dispassionate way and to sort them out as well and as quickly as you can. Certainly this should not be a long process because there are so many practical jobs around that also need your attention. Someone needs your timely advice, so keep your eyes open.

23 WEDNESDAY
Moon Age Day 24   Moon Sign Virgo

Remove yourself from the company of those who seem determined to be losers. This really isn't your way and it can only depress you if you are constantly surrounded by moaners. Of course you will do what you can to help everyone but you are less willing to do so in the case of those who won't assist themselves.

24 THURSDAY
Moon Age Day 25   Moon Sign Libra

Consider the present influences to be nothing more than a short layoff between more positive trends. Take time out to think about things and do your best to find enjoyment in low-key ways. Talking casually to people you really like is one way to avert your gaze from some of the apparent inadequacies around you.

25 FRIDAY   *Moon Age Day 26   Moon Sign Libra*

Beware of potential setbacks. The lunar low won't sap your resolve but it might prevent you from doing exactly what you would wish. In all probability you will find yourself being held back by circumstances beyond your own control. What cannot be altered must be endured. Once you realise this fact, you simply move on anyway.

26 SATURDAY   *Moon Age Day 27   Moon Sign Libra*

A minor personal letdown from a friend is something you will simply have to accept. The trends generally are very good, even though the lunar low is around for a day or two. This is the part of the month during which you are very good at thinking and planning, though less effective in a practical sense.

27 SUNDAY   *Moon Age Day 28   Moon Sign Scorpio*

Be careful that you are not becoming obsessed in any way. This is particularly true when it comes to emotional ties and especially so for young or unattached Arians. It isn't easy to be objective at the moment but there ought to be plenty of advice on hand if you are willing to look for it.

28 MONDAY   *Moon Age Day 29   Moon Sign Scorpio*

The situation regarding your career is somewhat complicated right now but there should be the promise of better things to come. Consider your options carefully and don't allow yourself to get drawn into discussions or arguments that have no purpose. Some discomfort can probably be expected from time to time today.

29 TUESDAY   *Moon Age Day 0   Moon Sign Sagittarius*

The lighter side of life appears to be what you are seeking at present. Contribute to the general hilarity that surrounds you at this time, though since you are creating most of it that should not be difficult. Money pressures are likely to ease and you could even find yourself to be better off than you thought.

30 WEDNESDAY *Moon Age Day 1   Moon Sign Sagittarius*

Your profile is high at present and that means that attention is still coming your way, sometimes from less than favourable directions. Not all situations will be perfect but the majority need to suit you and there isn't much point in pretending otherwise. Simply stay away from those who don't interest you at all.

December

2016

1 THURSDAY
Moon Age Day 2   Moon Sign Sagittarius

The start of the month is likely to bring an emotional issue that will require some careful handling on your part. Avoid getting yourself into a state over things that can be sorted out easily if you keep your cool. Thoughts of Christmas will probably be on your mind already, though they should be positive ones.

2 FRIDAY
Moon Age Day 3   Moon Sign Capricorn

You put a lot of energy into getting results and being generally busy. Of course this ensures that you get a great deal done but it will also cut down on the social time available. Exchange ideas, even with people you haven't altogether seen eye to eye with previously. By doing so you derive a new perspective.

3 SATURDAY
Moon Age Day 4   Moon Sign Capricorn

Your ability to handle several different tasks at the same time is clearly marked today. This is Aries working at its best and so a happy time can be expected. Actually life may be a blur of activity on occasions, though it appears you should still find the time to spend with those who are dear to you.

4 SUNDAY
Moon Age Day 5   Moon Sign Aquarius

Many issues can seem to be particularly fulfilling at the moment. Perhaps you now have a greater sense of financial security, or at the very least ideas that can bring it about. You are confident in your ability to do the right thing but be careful to side step the enquiries of a nosy friend.

5 MONDAY
Moon Age Day 6   Moon Sign Aquarius

It could appear that friendly meetings and even business associations only have something going for them today when they are massaging your ego, which isn't small at present. That's part of your astrological nature, but you do have the ability to at least attempt humility from time to time.

6 TUESDAY
Moon Age Day 7   Moon Sign Aquarius

It may be unwise to believe everything that you hear today. Although the majority of people are clearly doing what they can to tell you the truth, it may come down to being a matter of perspective at the end of the day. In other words nobody is deliberately trying to fool you, it simply seems that way.

7 WEDNESDAY
Moon Age Day 8   Moon Sign Pisces

In terms of work your ability to get ahead may be subject to a number of small setbacks. Don't worry if this turns out to be the case because it's clear that you have your sights set on personal and social matters. Even Aries can't be all things to all people for every moment of each day.

8 THURSDAY
Moon Age Day 9   Moon Sign Pisces

Your competitive side shows when you are involved in almost any sort of discussion. This would not be a good time to get too involved in sorting out the whole world however, since there is more than enough to do in your own life. Beware of spending too many hours simply proving other people wrong.

9 FRIDAY
Moon Age Day 10   Moon Sign Aries

The lunar high brings you to a physical and mental peak and the part of the month when you will really want to show what you are made of. The competitive edge begins to make itself felt and almost anything you do brings that Aries desire to win through, no matter what the opposition might be.

10 SATURDAY   *Moon Age Day 11   Moon Sign Aries*

You could talk the hind leg off a donkey right now. That's good, because you also have the ability to get on with just about anyone. The genuinely likeable quality of your Aries nature is on display, which ensures popularity. In turn this gives you more confidence and closes a necessary circle of self-belief for you.

11 SUNDAY   *Moon Age Day 12   Moon Sign Taurus*

Certain information is apt to go astray today, so it's important to watch what you are doing and to ask the right questions frequently. This state of affairs is down to short stay planetary influences so is a very fleeting phenomenon. Don't forget to support family members who are working hard now.

12 MONDAY   *Moon Age Day 13   Moon Sign Taurus*

There isn't much doubt that some issues can be turned easily to your advantage. Seeking these out isn't as easy today as is going to prove to be the case tomorrow. A good deal of thought needs to go into planning your next move, particularly at work. You should also now be really looking ahead towards Christmas.

13 TUESDAY   *Moon Age Day 14   Moon Sign Gemini*

The going is still very good when it comes to new incentives and alternative ways of looking at life. So capable are you today that it appears you have everything you need to mix business and pleasure in a totally successful sort of way. If you have been thinking about some new sort of regime, now is the time to get stuck in.

14 WEDNESDAY   *Moon Age Day 15   Moon Sign Gemini*

A professional matter can go astray, leaving you floundering for an hour or two. If this turns out to be the case simply turn on all that practical Aries energy and pull yourself out of the problem. Socially speaking you are especially good company and should find your popularity extremely well accented now.

15 THURSDAY   *Moon Age Day 16   Moon Sign Cancer*

This is an ideal period to try to broaden your horizons. Be careful what you take on though because Christmas is just around the corner and you don't want incentives to flag during the festive season. What might be best of all is to plan a strategy that commences almost at the start of the new year.

16 FRIDAY   *Moon Age Day 17   Moon Sign Cancer*

It is one thing to be optimistic and quite another to believe that you can move mountains. What is called for now is a dose of realism, though allied to incentive and belief. If you can strike this happy medium there is almost nothing beyond your abilities. Romance seems to be knocking at any time now.

17 SATURDAY   *Moon Age Day 18   Moon Sign Leo*

Pleasure pursuits and romantic issues are interesting you greatly at present. Some practical issues might also be coming to a head and you will want to do everything you can to encourage your own eventual success. That's fine but don't push too hard when life itself is in a position to help you out.

18 SUNDAY   *Moon Age Day 19   Moon Sign Leo*

A strong sense of restlessness strikes home for some Aries subjects at present. This could be a reaction to the fact that social trends seem ruled by Christmas, something that probably won't suit you down to the ground. Look out for some sort of adventure and try to ring the changes in terms of social events.

19 MONDAY   *Moon Age Day 20   Moon Sign Virgo*

This should prove to be a day for smooth professional progress, even if not everyone appears to be exactly on your side just for the moment. That's partly because you are more than willing to make a competition out of events that are not important at all. Don't defend yourself if you are not attacked.

20 TUESDAY ☿ *Moon Age Day 21 Moon Sign Virgo*

Some of you are going to be so busy on the social scene today that it becomes impossible to approach practical issues with quite the gusto you might wish. Never mind, what isn't sorted today can be dealt with later. In all probability you are so very active simply because Christmas is only a few days away.

21 WEDNESDAY ☿ *Moon Age Day 22 Moon Sign Virgo*

You should enjoy almost anything that life is throwing at you now. With a good sense of proportion, winning ways and a determination to end up at the front, you push on regardless. People love the fact that you don't give in, even on those rare occasions when the odds seem to be stacked against you.

22 THURSDAY ☿ *Moon Age Day 23 Moon Sign Libra*

Unfortunately some people are getting ahead faster than you are just now. There is little or nothing that you can do about this situation, at least not without wearing yourself out altogether. Why not show a greater willingness to let those around you do some of the work, whilst you take a backseat for once?

23 FRIDAY ☿ *Moon Age Day 24 Moon Sign Libra*

There are influences around today that can perk up your social and personal life no end, even though at the start of the day you will find the lunar low still in operation. By lunchtime it isn't hard to find yourself working and playing hard again, and finally looking forward to what lies in store in the days ahead.

24 SATURDAY ☿ *Moon Age Day 25 Moon Sign Scorpio*

On a personal level you are feeling rather competitive. There's nothing at all new about that from an Aries perspective, though it's rather pointless proving your worth to people who recognise it well already. By the evening you should be more than willing to let your hair down and have some real fun.

25 SUNDAY ☿ *Moon Age Day 26* *Moon Sign Scorpio*

A great Christmas Day is in the offing, even if you begin to run out of steam later in the day. Trends are variable and show you to be open-minded, well able to get on with a variety of different types and enjoying life to the full. Some of the surprises that come your way today should be especially delightful.

26 MONDAY ☿ *Moon Age Day 27* *Moon Sign Scorpio*

Now you find yourself faced with another eventful and generally positive sort of day. With people constantly trying to gain your attention it could be somewhat difficult to please everyone, though you are certain to try. Family and friends are the ones who tend to win out as far as you are concerned now.

27 TUESDAY ☿ *Moon Age Day 28* *Moon Sign Sagittarius*

Beware of a fairly up and down period where work is concerned, though of course if you are not at work this trend is hardly likely to have a bearing on your day. Certainly from a social point of view you look and feel good. Although you can't have quite everything you want romantically now, you won't fall far short.

28 WEDNESDAY ☿ *Moon Age Day 29* *Moon Sign Sagittarius*

Though eager to get your ideas across, you will be rather too anxious to spread the word at this time. The fact is that you are likely to scare some people off, especially if you have to deal with types who are far less gregarious than you are. Slow and steady wins some sort of race that has social overtones.

29 THURSDAY ☿ *Moon Age Day 0* *Moon Sign Capricorn*

Work matters are likely to keep you on the go at this time. If, on the other hand, you are away from work until after the new year, you are likely to be busy on the home front. Enjoying yourself can be tiring, which is why you need to turn your mind in more practical directions if possible.

30 FRIDAY ☿ *Moon Age Day 1* *Moon Sign Capricorn*

For the first time since Christmas you could be quite happy to be away from the crowds for a few hours. Although there are things to do that make you appear quieter than usual, at least take some time out to let those around you know that you are not sulking about something. Extra effort with relatives is especially important.

31 SATURDAY ☿ *Moon Age Day 2* *Moon Sign Capricorn*

The last day of the year offers you the chance to make a very positive social impact on the world at large. Aries is in the mood to party and there are people around who should be more than willing to join in. Don't take yourself or anyone else too seriously for the moment and concentrate on having fun.

ARIES:
2017 DIARY PAGES

ARIES:
YOUR YEAR IN BRIEF

It's important to start the year as you mean to go on, even if you feel a little lacking in vitality as things get started. January and February bring positive trends and a desire to get ahead, no matter what the price. There are financial gains to be made and you have plenty of incentive to work at relationships. Rules and regulations may be irritating, but should not hinder your desire to keep pushing forward. Aries is good at beating the odds in any situation.

You are willing to do almost anything you can to help others and to take on board new challenges at every turn. This is particularly obvious in the earliest days of spring. March and April may bring some financial and professional success, but even this is partly due to the good offices of others, helped by your own attitude. Take a little care when it comes to expenditure and don't go further than is strictly sensible at this time.

May and June will find you really waking up to the advancing year. This is a time to make progress at work and also a period to make some surprising new friendships. You won't tolerate routines and you will be quite happy to ring the changes in your life whenever and wherever possible. Stand by for new responsibilities in May.

July and August are definitely months for love. Throughout both you will be looking at relationships in a new light and doing all you can to strengthen your commitment and prove how steadfast and reliable you can be. Take any opportunity to overthrow normal boundaries and allow your unique personality to shine through. Avoid family arguments at this time but don't always do what is strictly expected of you. Make plenty of time for travel, especially during August.

Both September and October have a great deal to offer in terms of variety. You still feel the need to ring the changes whenever possible and you will soon get bored if everything remains the same from day to day. The attitude of friends and in particular loved ones could be mystifying, so it's just as well your intuition is turned up to full at this time. Some financial gains are indicated during the middle and towards the end of October.

November and December are a slightly mixed bag. November is likely to be slow to start and may be a little frustrating at times, but things will soon start to liven up. By the end of the month you will be firing on all cylinders and anxious to make the best of impressions. December could be the most progressive month of the year and is good for love, financial gain and establishing new attachments in every area of your life.

January 2017

1 SUNDAY ☿ *Moon Age Day 4 Moon Sign Aquarius*

You begin the year in an insightful mood and with a good ability to express yourself. It may benefit you to share your thoughts and ideas with trusted friends or with your partner. Intuition is not something Arians rely on very often, but you are certainly in the market to do so during much of this month.

2 MONDAY ☿ *Moon Age Day 5 Moon Sign Aquarius*

Be aware that today you could encounter conflict with people who usually give you no trouble at all. You will need to be tactful and to let your friends know you are there to support them when it matters the most. Settle down to routines but also push on towards important goals if you can.

3 TUESDAY ☿ *Moon Age Day 6 Moon Sign Pisces*

Utilise your natural energy and zest for life in your approach today and you might leave others standing. This side of your nature is really on display at present and you have everything it takes to make the best of impressions. If you are going out this evening, do your best to take someone along who you really like.

4 WEDNESDAY ☿ *Moon Age Day 7 Moon Sign Pisces*

Keep any tendency to self-important behaviour at bay and make certain that you don't brag or come across as being in any way arrogant. Instead, prove how humble and self-effacing you can be and the world will be your oyster. You are naturally dominant so don't expect to find it easy to let others take the lead.

73

5 THURSDAY   ☿   *Moon Age Day 8   Moon Sign Aries*

Keep pushing because you are likely to have the best of everything coming your way at this stage of the working week. Arians who have experienced difficulties in the recent past should now find that these troublesome matters are resolved. You might notice that the way others perceive you has become a whole lot more positive.

6 FRIDAY   ☿   *Moon Age Day 9   Moon Sign Aries*

Enjoy your ability to get things done at lightning speed, perhaps with a little luck on your side. There are times when it would be prudent to stop, look and listen but this is hardly likely to be the case during this lunar high. They say that fools rush in where angels fear to tread, but there are times when a lucky fool can really succeed.

7 SATURDAY   ☿   *Moon Age Day 10   Moon Sign Taurus*

Look forward to a chance to expand your circle of contacts at the moment and use your new acquaintances to your advantage. Despite any adverse winter weather, today could be good for getting out and about and you should be able to find a way to bring some spring warmth into the day.

8 SUNDAY   *Moon Age Day 11   Moon Sign Taurus*

Philosophy, culture and travel will all appeal to you under present planetary trends. Aries people who have the chance to get away from routines now or in the near future should grab the opportunity with both hands. Even if you have to stay at home and keep working you can still do things in a varied and more interesting way.

9 MONDAY   *Moon Age Day 12   Moon Sign Gemini*

Today you need to be the master of your own destiny and you certainly won't take kindly to being told what to do by people you consider to be misinformed. Bear in mind that there are times when it is prudent co-operate with others. It is far better now to watch and wait than to react too quickly and to cause problems for yourself later.

10 TUESDAY   *Moon Age Day 13   Moon Sign Gemini*

Be careful that some of your expectations today don't end with unnecessary regret. Stay realistic and be willing to compromise at any stage if you sense that this is the best way forward. Bashing your head against a brick wall is definitely not to be recommended and will mean an obvious headache which could be avoided.

11 WEDNESDAY   *Moon Age Day 14   Moon Sign Cancer*

Make this a day of honesty – but only up to a certain point. There are a few people around who might not be up to facing the truth as you see it and for them it will be necessary to approach reality in easy stages. A little diplomacy can go a long way and can make sure you retain the popularity that is very important to you.

12 THURSDAY   *Moon Age Day 15   Moon Sign Cancer*

Make sure everyone understands what you are saying and why. This means being clear and concise in your communications, whilst at the same time going into detail if necessary. Don't get too tied down with the problems of others except in those cases when you are sure you have the answers at your fingertips.

13 FRIDAY   *Moon Age Day 16   Moon Sign Cancer*

The current position of the planets in your chart does not favour a lot of intense concentration, so expect to struggle a little with any tasks which actually require in-depth thought. Even your choice of reading matter at the moment is likely to be trivial and funny.

14 SATURDAY   *Moon Age Day 17   Moon Sign Leo*

Exciting people are likely to come into your life this weekend and it is clear that any confusion or concern of the last couple of days is now out of the way. Make the most of all new situations and allow that active mind of yours to concentrate on what lies around every new and interesting corner. Make this a fun weekend.

15 SUNDAY   *Moon Age Day 18   Moon Sign Leo*

Giving yourself fully to almost anything that takes your fancy is what this particular Sunday is all about. At the same time you will show yourself able to work long and hard on behalf of your partner, a family member or even a good friend. Everyone you meet seems to be filled with good ideas, some of which you will want to adopt.

16 MONDAY   *Moon Age Day 19   Moon Sign Virgo*

There is likely to be plenty of assistance around today when you need it the most but you might have trouble realising it. It would be very easy to go further and further down a road that leads to nowhere, which is precisely why you ought to be opening your mind to a different point of view. Family members may be demanding today.

17 TUESDAY   *Moon Age Day 20   Moon Sign Virgo*

For once you could be quite humble in your attitude – a fact that could surprise more than one person in your vicinity at the moment. Not everyone is equally good to know at present and the planetary line-up could bring you into contact with those who are deeply authoritative in attitude and who rely heavily on red tape.

18 WEDNESDAY   *Moon Age Day 21   Moon Sign Libra*

The Moon now moves into Libra, bringing that period known as the lunar low. You need to be quite careful in the way you go about doing almost anything for today and tomorrow and might easily be feeling dejected or tired. This is a natural process and one that may not bother you at all once you realise that it is a temporary state of affairs.

19 THURSDAY   *Moon Age Day 22   Moon Sign Libra*

You are facing a planetary red light and there isn't much to be done except to watch and wait. By taking any real action at this time you are only going to cause problems for yourself further down the line, which is why it would be sensible to have a rest and to build a few personal bridges. In a day or two you will be back to normal.

20 FRIDAY
Moon Age Day 23   Moon Sign Scorpio

Social developments may take an interesting turn and there isn't much doubt that you are looking closely at intriguing information that is coming your way all the time. Your confidence in your ability to do the right thing is not lacking and now that the lunar low is out of the way you should be able to race forward and show great enterprise.

21 SATURDAY
Moon Age Day 24   Moon Sign Scorpio

The present position of the Sun fills you with a desire to be with people you like and to discuss matters that are not simply side issues or chit-chat. Not everyone you meet will have quite your depth, so expect to have to deal with individuals who have a radically different view of life to yours. Flexibility is the key to success now.

22 SUNDAY
Moon Age Day 25   Moon Sign Scorpio

You continue to look at life in an optimistic way and that means there are happy times to be had. Although the winter weather might be slightly depressing you can find things to do that are not impeded by any sleet or snow. Find somewhere warm to go and also do what you can to stimulate your more intellectual side.

23 MONDAY
Moon Age Day 26   Moon Sign Sagittarius

It looks as though you will not be keen to involve yourself in any unnecessary work, especially if it would mean a great deal of physical effort. However, things are likely to change rapidly tomorrow – all the more reason to get plans sorted out and to work out how to achieve something that has been on your mind of late.

24 TUESDAY
Moon Age Day 27   Moon Sign Sagittarius

When it comes to progress today you are clearly guided by your feelings and intuition but you won't stand around waiting for messages to come in. On the contrary your reactions are lightning quick and you are unlikely to put a foot wrong. You should also be in a competitive mood and won't like to lose.

25 WEDNESDAY   *Moon Age Day 28   Moon Sign Capricorn*

Do your best to slow down the pace of life today because it is more than possible that some issues are running away with you. This is not likely to be the case in terms of romance because things could hardly be working better for you in this sphere of your life. You know exactly what to say in order to sweep someone off their feet.

26 THURSDAY   *Moon Age Day 29   Moon Sign Capricorn*

Good company is not hard to find at present and this period should turn out to be a cracker from a social point of view. You have what it takes at the moment to mix business with pleasure and it is possible that someone who has been little more than a colleague in the past will turn out to be very much more in the future.

27 FRIDAY   *Moon Age Day 0   Moon Sign Capricorn*

Beware of too many emotional drives playing out in your life at the same time. You could be deeply attached to more than one individual, though there is probably also a great sense of responsibility involved. This could cloud your judgement. You will almost certainly come to the conclusion that something will have to be toned down.

28 SATURDAY   *Moon Age Day 1   Moon Sign Aquarius*

If you have to deal with slightly unpleasant confrontations today it would be best to get these out of the way as early in the day as you can. At least that way you won't dwell on situations for too long and can then concentrate on more pleasant matters. Friends are likely to be getting in touch with you all through the day.

29 SUNDAY   *Moon Age Day 2   Moon Sign Aquarius*

This is likely to be a Sunday that both surprises and delights you. Easy confidence abounds, and it seems as though practically everyone you meet is happy to fall in line with your ideas. Don't be too sure of yourself, though, because even for Aries too much pride is not a good thing. Friends continue to be inspirational today.

30 MONDAY
Moon Age Day 3   Moon Sign Pisces

New commitments should be just the job because you almost always relish the chance to do something different. Today offers the possibility of travel and should certainly introduce you to new people and situations that are fresh and appealing. What you don't need right now are friends who are so demanding that they depress you.

31 TUESDAY
Moon Age Day 4   Moon Sign Pisces

When it comes to meeting new people you are clearly in your element at the moment. At the same time you will be giving a good deal of energy to personal attachments. It may occur to you that things on the romantic front are becoming a little routine and you might feel inspired to do something to liven them up.

February

2017

1 WEDNESDAY
Moon Age Day 5   Moon Sign Aries

Any previous concerns you may have had about your limitations are out of the window now as the Moon races into your own zodiac sign. The lunar high will see you overflowing with energy and positively determined to make a splash in life generally. Friends find you electric and your popularity leaps ahead.

2 THURSDAY
Moon Age Day 6   Moon Sign Aries

You have the capacity to occupy a high-profile position at the moment and show a real desire to push the bounds of possibility. Few could fail to notice your self-confidence or your willingness to have fun. With your leadership skills on full display at present, others will be happy to follow your lead.

3 FRIDAY
Moon Age Day 7   Moon Sign Aries

Things are still likely to be fairly hectic but there could be a couple of quieter days on the way so you can afford to put in that extra bit of effort now that might make all the difference. Romance looks good, especially for Arians who have recently begun a new relationship or else re-visited an old one.

4 SATURDAY
Moon Age Day 8   Moon Sign Taurus

Commitment is the key to success now and you should not be afraid to nail your colours to any mast that is important to you. There isn't much mileage in being half-hearted, particularly when it comes to workplace situations. Even if you sometimes make the wrong decisions, rest assured that you will find ways and means to triumph anyway.

5 SUNDAY
Moon Age Day 9   Moon Sign Taurus

This could turn out to be one of the very best days of the month as far as relationships are concerned. It is easy for you to find exactly the right words to say in order to sweep someone off their feet, and romantic attachments are likely to look especially good under present planetary trends. Relatives could be a little awkward now.

6 MONDAY
Moon Age Day 10   Moon Sign Gemini

If you overcome a slight tendency to jump to irrational conclusions today you will probably do yourself a great deal of good. Enjoying harmonious relationships with others is now partly dependent on being willing to compromise – something that doesn't always come easily to you. It's plain that extra effort is required.

7 TUESDAY
Moon Age Day 11   Moon Sign Gemini

It looks as though you are embarking on a period of renewal and there are strong planetary supports for any new effort you make at the moment. Not everything is going to go the way you would wish but when it matters the most you have what it takes to put in that extra bit of effort that can make all the difference.

8 WEDNESDAY
Moon Age Day 12   Moon Sign Cancer

Close ties are positively cemented under present planetary trends and you show today just how loyal you can be. A good percentage of your time is likely to be spent supporting others and you are fair in your attitude to life generally. This is Aries at its best and you can be fairly certain that you are being noticed by all manner of people.

9 THURSDAY
Moon Age Day 13   Moon Sign Cancer

Aries the perfectionist is on display this weekend and you are unlikely to embark on any project unless you are sure that you can see it through to a positive conclusion. The only slight problem is that you may spend so much time getting things right that you miss a few other opportunities that are waiting in the wings.

10 FRIDAY
Moon Age Day 14   Moon Sign Leo

Today would be an entirely appropriate time to get rid of some of the dead wood from your life. Although in a general sense it is a little early yet for spring cleaning, the process of altering things to make your life less cluttered is commencing and you won't take kindly to any more junk being offloaded on to you.

11 SATURDAY
Moon Age Day 15   Moon Sign Leo

Intellectual and philosophical interests are very important this Saturday and you are keen to improve your mind in any way that proves possible. Communication is also significant and you may be receiving letters, emails or texts that carry important information. You will certainly have some good ideas up your sleeve now.

12 SUNDAY
Moon Age Day 16   Moon Sign Virgo

If there is one thing you seem to be looking for today it is security. Anything you can do to make yourself feel more comfortable and to bolster your financial resources for the future is grist to the mill at the moment. There are quieter times in store so you do need to remain generally active today and to get things done quickly.

13 MONDAY
Moon Age Day 17   Moon Sign Virgo

The focus during the first part of this week is clearly going to be on your social life and though you continue to work hard in a professional sense, it is having fun that interests you most. You might feel confident enough at the moment to fly off to somewhere exotic and even if you can't your mind wanders far and wide.

14 TUESDAY
Moon Age Day 18   Moon Sign Libra

The lunar low could take the wind out of your sails a little today and it will almost certainly make it more difficult for you to achieve all your objectives. It would be better to show a little patience and to accept that rest is also a natural part of life. Curl up in a comfortable chair with a good book and wait for a day or two.

15 WEDNESDAY   *Moon Age Day 19   Moon Sign Libra*

There are likely to be a few financial fluctuations about – yet another gift of the lunar low – though these are not likely to be serious or long lasting. Friends might be rather difficult to deal with, especially if they think you might have been ignoring them of late. A special effort might be necessary but do you have the energy now?

16 THURSDAY   *Moon Age Day 20   Moon Sign Libra*

Whilst the Sun remains in your solar eleventh house you can use this trend to gain fulfilment through friendships. Certain people will be very important to you at the moment and you shouldn't have any difficulty making new pals around now. If there are any parties in the offing, this is the time to seek out an invitation.

17 FRIDAY   *Moon Age Day 21   Moon Sign Scorpio*

Though you are probably not known for your tact or diplomacy you do have what it takes to pour oil on troubled waters at the moment. This could be the case at work, or at home where certain family members are refusing to see eye-to-eye. In love you show a very passionate approach that won't be lost on your partner.

18 SATURDAY   *Moon Age Day 22   Moon Sign Scorpio*

Some of your present views could be at odds with the wider world and there may be a need to go it alone, at least for a short while. You don't mind being out on a limb – just as long as you are certain that your point of view is valid. Your present attitude will get you noticed but perhaps on occasion for the wrong reasons.

19 SUNDAY   *Moon Age Day 23   Moon Sign Sagittarius*

It is your social life that should provide the best moments this Sunday and you will probably be doing all you can to pep things up. At the same time you show yourself to be very competitive and will be eagerly joining in sporting activities or pastimes that have a rowdy or an energetic aspect. This is not a good time to gamble.

20 MONDAY *Moon Age Day 24 Moon Sign Sagittarius*

Pleasing everybody today could prove to be a hopeless task so maybe you would be better off sticking to those people you care for the most. At work you are likely to be at odds with certain individuals and may feel inclined to 'tell it how it is' even if this means you could fall out with one or two people. Tread carefully all the same.

21 TUESDAY *Moon Age Day 25 Moon Sign Sagittarius*

Concentrate a good deal of your energy today on your love life. You will be surprised just how important a kind word can be, not to mention a spontaneous gesture. These put you in the good books of others and also make you feel good about yourself. Your level of general luck is likely to be higher so you can afford to take a chance.

22 WEDNESDAY *Moon Age Day 26 Moon Sign Capricorn*

You won't find a better time this month for sorting out your life and improving your efficiency. The need for spring-cleaning comes early for Aries this year and although the cold weather may still be around, you should also be feeling the call of the great outdoors. A brisk walk in the park or a stroll up a hill would do you good.

23 THURSDAY *Moon Age Day 27 Moon Sign Capricorn*

You really do want to get out and explore the world at present and the position of Mercury in your solar chart also makes you chatty and sociable. Things are better when done in groups and you won't be so inclined to take command. Co-operation is the key word and a greater desire to share is attaching itself to Aries generally.

24 FRIDAY *Moon Age Day 28 Moon Sign Aquarius*

This is a busy social phase and a time when friends both motivate and please you by their actions. Show everyone how much you care because Aries is sometimes a little lax in this department. You need to actively force yourself to offer compliments because not everyone is aware of how fond of them you actually are.

25 SATURDAY
Moon Age Day 0   Moon Sign Aquarius

Focus on professional matters if you work at the weekend but if you don't it's worthwhile planning ahead to next week. The way certain other people do things is apt to frustrate you somewhat but you should be able to lend a hand without appearing to be too pushy. Material concerns are important now but don't forget friendship.

26 SUNDAY
Moon Age Day 1   Moon Sign Aquarius

Your love life should keep you feeling on top of the world and there isn't much that is beyond you when it comes to handing out the right compliment at the right time. Spend as much time as you can in the company of your lover and at the same time show family members that you care about them more than they might think.

27 MONDAY
Moon Age Day 2   Moon Sign Pisces

You have the ability to be an organiser this week and although there isn't anything particularly unusual about this for Aries, your skills in this direction are even greater than usual. That is why you may be called upon to stand in for someone senior and also why you simply adopt the position of team leader at the drop of a hat.

28 TUESDAY
Moon Age Day 3   Moon Sign Pisces

There are past issues to be dealt with today so you need to look carefully at the way you behaved before and modify your approach if necessary. With plenty of diplomacy on your side you can bring others round to your point of view and should be especially good at sorting out difficult issues amongst colleagues or friends.

March

1 WEDNESDAY
Moon Age Day 4   Moon Sign Aries

It is vital for you now to be where the action is and to keep trying, even when others have fallen by the wayside. Other people should look to you as group leader and you won't have to work too hard in order to get what you want from life. Focus your attention on certain situations that require your competitive edge.

2 THURSDAY
Moon Age Day 5   Moon Sign Aries

This ought to be a very successful time for Aries and if it isn't you probably are not working hard enough. Life offers you new incentives and all you really have to do is accept them when they come along. Making gains at the moment is a little like picking fruit and Lady Luck is likely to play a part in your day.

3 FRIDAY
Moon Age Day 6   Moon Sign Taurus

Don't be lulled into a false sense of security just because of what others are telling you. This is a time when you need to look at matters for yourself and to turn over a few stones if necessary. You have your Sherlock Holmes hat on and though your attitude might amuse some of your friends it turns out to be worthwhile.

4 SATURDAY
Moon Age Day 7   Moon Sign Taurus

Places you are likely to be visiting today give you new incentives and feed your imagination no end. This is why you really do need to move around at the moment and to avoid being stuck at home where nothing much is likely to be happening. Once again you have the opportunity to support someone who is important to you.

5 SUNDAY
Moon Age Day 8   Moon Sign Gemini

This is a time for renovations and for putting yourself to the test. It looks as though there are some cracking opportunities coming your way and you won't want to be left at the starting post in a race for new possibilities. This is especially true when it comes to changes you want to make in and around your home.

6 MONDAY
Moon Age Day 9   Moon Sign Gemini

The present planetary trends ought to broaden your horizons no end, which with the slightly better weather and the lighter nights make you more cheerful and committed. From a professional point of view you could now be taking on new responsibilities with some Aries subjects even contemplating a total change of career.

7 TUESDAY
Moon Age Day 10   Moon Sign Cancer

New personalities are likely to be entering your life at any time now and this should make for an interested and varied social life. Those closest to you can be a little difficult to deal with and this is most likely to be the case with younger family members. Fortunately, thanks to some positive planetary trends you remain calm.

8 WEDNESDAY
Moon Age Day 11   Moon Sign Cancer

All communications and travel-related matters are grist to the mill for Aries right now and it seems as though your energy is without end. 'Seems' is the appropriate word here because like everyone else you do have your limits. Make sure that periods of high activity are balanced by other times when you can genuinely relax.

9 THURSDAY
Moon Age Day 12   Moon Sign Leo

The emphasis at the moment is on personal freedom above all else so take the chance to do those things that please you. What won't please you very much at the moment are the expectations that others have of you, especially in a domestic sense. The slightest feeling that you are being taken for granted could see you going on strike!

10 FRIDAY
Moon Age Day 13   Moon Sign Leo

Aries is especially curious at the moment and you could spend a good part of today turning over stones, simply to see what lies beneath them. Satisfying yourself as to the mechanisms of life is not unusual but what may be rather different is the use to which you put some of your discoveries. You have a great capacity for original thought.

11 SATURDAY
Moon Age Day 14   Moon Sign Virgo

This is a weekend during which your thirst for personal freedom appears to know no bounds. Together with friends you can accomplish much and you will be very charitable in your general attitude at the present time. If there is a problem here it is the very slight possibility that you might sometimes appear condescending.

12 SUNDAY
Moon Age Day 15   Moon Sign Virgo

The progress you make now appears to have no limits but beware because things could grind to a definite halt by Tuesday. For this reason it would be best to finish what you start today, so that you can enter the lunar low with the feeling that there is nothing crucial that remains outstanding. Arrange for a relaxing evening to end the weekend.

13 MONDAY
Moon Age Day 16   Moon Sign Virgo

Focus as much as you can right now on professional matters because this is the part of the month when you can genuinely make progress. In social settings you show yourself to be a real personality and almost everyone will be pleased to have you around. Something you have been waiting for is now likely to happen.

14 TUESDAY
Moon Age Day 17   Moon Sign Libra

You might be forgiven for believing that a good deal of what is happening around you today is very low-key. This is the gift of the lunar low, which is inclined to take the wind out of your sails somewhat. People around you will be less than helpful and in the end you may have to abandon something, at least for the moment.

15 WEDNESDAY   *Moon Age Day 18   Moon Sign Libra*

Drop the reins of control for a few hours and let others work on your behalf. Meanwhile you can find interesting ways and means of entertaining yourself, just as long as whatever you choose doesn't demand a great deal of energy. Get in touch with friends later in the day and think about an evening of quiet fun.

16 THURSDAY   *Moon Age Day 19   Moon Sign Scorpio*

As if by magic the horizons clear for you and suddenly you are once again fully in command of your own life. You may have to make some important career decisions at this time and if so you should be willing to listen to the advice of someone who is in the know. Co-operation becomes a keyword between now and the weekend.

17 FRIDAY   *Moon Age Day 20   Moon Sign Scorpio*

Forward-moving trends become obvious and in a domestic sense at least you will probably be seeking new starts and significant changes. You might be faced once again with the need to assess certain people in new ways and though eating humble pie is not something that Aries enjoys, this too might be necessary.

18 SATURDAY   *Moon Age Day 21   Moon Sign Scorpio*

Social arrangements now tend to get rerouted and you need to be able to think on your feet if you are to avoid a fairly complicated sort of day. If you are at work you should be giving your best but there are possible problems coming from the direction of colleagues. Maybe they don't fully understand what you are trying to tell them.

19 SUNDAY   *Moon Age Day 22   Moon Sign Sagittarius*

A great deal of your life this Sunday is likely to centre on communication and the chance to get your message across to others in a very positive way. You may not have to plan everything in a moment-by-moment sense and in fact will do rather better if you simply react to situations that are taking place around you.

20 MONDAY *Moon Age Day 23   Moon Sign Sagittarius*

A thirst for knowledge and a need to open up your personal horizons also means you will want to travel around this time. Maybe it isn't possible for you to drop everything and fly off to some exotic location but even small journeys can prove to be a real boon. And when you can't travel in the flesh you can do so in your mind.

21 TUESDAY *Moon Age Day 24   Moon Sign Capricorn*

You need to apply some realism to your thoughts and ideas, especially as far as home and family are concerned. There are certain aspects of life that cannot be the same as they used to be and although it is always comfortable to stick to what you know, once things alter for the better you can re-establish a new familiar routine.

22 WEDNESDAY *Moon Age Day 25   Moon Sign Capricorn*

Career responsibilities could provide you with many challenges. Life demands leadership and initiative from you and you won't have any problem providing both. You are more than up to any task you choose to take on, though there could be occasions when you are trying to achieve the impossible.

23 THURSDAY *Moon Age Day 26   Moon Sign Capricorn*

You can be the main attraction in social groups and you continue to show how much you have to offer your family and friends. What is most gratifying about this period is that despite the fact you remain generally busy you will find moments to support and if necessary comfort other people. Get outings organised now for next weekend.

24 FRIDAY *Moon Age Day 27   Moon Sign Aquarius*

Now you tend to meet the sort of people you will appreciate for their wisdom and their ability to help you out. Take advantage of situations that come your way and don't be left on the starting post when there is any race to run. It might be difficult to get yourself into the right frame of mind but it's important to participate fully.

25 SATURDAY   *Moon Age Day 28   Moon Sign Aquarius*

You tend to take your intellectual development more seriously this weekend and will be open to new ideas and possibilities that feed your mind. Of course like everything else this can go too far, and there are occasions when you could give yourself a headache or find it difficult to sleep. Meditation is important too.

26 SUNDAY   *Moon Age Day 29   Moon Sign Pisces*

You tend to be very impressionable at this stage of the weekend and also more inclined to have a bruised ego if you take offhand remarks too literally. This isn't a good reflection of your general nature but you are rather more sensitive than usual under present astrological trends and will need to shield your ego somewhat.

27 MONDAY   *Moon Age Day 0   Moon Sign Pisces*

Although it might seem less than likely on a normal working Monday the planets show that social get-togethers are going to be particularly rewarding. Maybe these will happen after work but wherever they come from they can bring great joy into your life. Don't allow pessimism to creep into your working life or strategies.

28 TUESDAY   *Moon Age Day 1   Moon Sign Aries*

As is often the case you are more than willing to accept the accolades that come your way but you do so in such a pleasant and magnanimous way that nobody begrudges you your successes. You might not think of yourself as being a generally lucky individual but a great deal seems to be going your way just at the moment.

29 WEDNESDAY   *Moon Age Day 2   Moon Sign Aries*

Look for people you don't see very often and, if the mood takes you, seek out those you haven't met at all for a number of years. Of course they will seem to have grown far older than you have and that fact at least will please you! Many of the comments you make at the moment are likely to be deliberately tongue-in-cheek.

30 THURSDAY
Moon Age Day 3   Moon Sign Taurus

This is a time when you will gain from friendships and you may even discover some unexpected allies. At work you should be putting things together in a very clever way and no matter what you do for a living it is likely that bosses will see you and your work in a very positive light. Advancement is possible.

31 FRIDAY
Moon Age Day 4   Moon Sign Taurus

Today you can be very amusing and won't have any difficulty in getting people to like you. In one or two cases this could even lead to a little embarrassment if the impression you make is rather greater than you imagined. Your general persona creates a positive attitude all round and you are showing the world your most positive face.

April

2017

1 SATURDAY
Moon Age Day 5   Moon Sign Gemini

There could be some scope for a few shortcuts to success at the moment, mainly because your attitude is so positive and people are happy to help you along. Whatever the request you should find someone who is willing to lend you a hand and this is only fair really because you do a great deal for others in a day-to-day sense.

2 SUNDAY
Moon Age Day 6   Moon Sign Gemini

This would not be a sensible time during which to believe everything you hear. As an Aries person you don't generally deal in gossip but there are occasions when others bend your ear and you do like a chat. You need to distinguish now between what might only be rumour and those remarks that are intended to deceive.

3 MONDAY
Moon Age Day 7   Moon Sign Cancer

The chances are that you will now be chatty, happy to go with the flow and just pleased with the lighter nights and the better weather. For some Arians it's as if you are waking up fully after a long sleep because your eyes are now opened to a whole series of new possibilities brought to light by the advancing year.

4 TUESDAY
Moon Age Day 8   Moon Sign Cancer

What you don't need right now are the sort of distractions that come about as a result of the vacillating tendencies of colleagues or even friends. You remain determined to forge ahead with your plans and will do so even if it means upsetting someone a little. In your reasoning this is acceptable because it is for their own good in the long run.

93

5 WEDNESDAY
Moon Age Day 9   Moon Sign Leo

Domestic or family conflicts could demand a good deal of your attention at present and you may have to spend a good deal of your time trying to calm people down. From your own point of view you can't really see why people were disagreeing in the first place but you will at least play the honest broker and try to see all points of view.

6 THURSDAY
Moon Age Day 10   Moon Sign Leo

Today is mostly about expressing yourself and it relies heavily on your ability and willingness to speak out for your own good. If this puts you into conflict with your partner or family members you can at least rely on your diplomacy, which is strong at present. Continue your efforts towards making necessary changes within your home.

7 FRIDAY
Moon Age Day 11   Moon Sign Leo

Today marks another good time for communicating with friends and for getting on well with everyone – even strangers. Your cheery attitude gets you noticed and you should find yourself in the company of like-minded people. This is Aries at its brightest and sunniest and the world at large seems thirsty for your company.

8 SATURDAY
Moon Age Day 12   Moon Sign Virgo

Your efforts out there in the wider world can now be helped no end if you make the right contacts in the first place. Seek out people who are experts in their field and listen carefully to what they have to say. Although the attitude of a friend might surprise you, you may come to see their point of view.

9 SUNDAY
Moon Age Day 13   Moon Sign Virgo

This Sunday has plenty to offer, though you may decide to slow things down and spend at least part of today concentrating on family matters and the people who are most important in your life. At the same time you could benefit from a shopping spree, in the company of someone who keeps you laughing.

10 MONDAY   ☿   *Moon Age Day 14   Moon Sign Libra*

It is more or less inevitable today that things will slow down and that you may be unable to get everything you want from a particular situation. It's a strange thing but when life was hectic a few days ago you showed a great deal of patience. Now, when you really need it the most, you seem to have a great lack of that particular virtue.

11 TUESDAY   ☿   *Moon Age Day 15   Moon Sign Libra*

The lunar low continues to influence almost every facet of your life today and you seem to have little choice but to react to situations, rather than instigating them yourself. Don't worry, in a day or so things will look very different and in the meantime you are left with some fairly solitary moments that can also be beneficial.

12 WEDNESDAY ☿   *Moon Age Day 16   Moon Sign Scorpio*

Make this a fulfilling time socially by reacting positively to invitations that are coming your way. You won't be so busy that you can't stop for a while and enjoy the positive social trends that are around. On the contrary, there are great gains to be made by those amongst you who are willing to mix business with pleasure.

13 THURSDAY   ☿   *Moon Age Day 17   Moon Sign Scorpio*

Friendships have much going for them right now and you might be quite willing to drop the reins of responsibility altogether in favour of simply enjoying yourself. A day out would suit you down to the ground. It doesn't much matter where you decide to go because it is the change of scenery and the sense of excitement that counts.

14 FRIDAY   ☿   *Moon Age Day 18   Moon Sign Scorpio*

Now you are more inclined to buckle down and to look more carefully and seriously at business interests. There are likely to be discussions regarding future security and trends suggest that you may have an important document to sign. Right now you can rely on your own good sense, as well as on some very specific and pointed advice.

15 SATURDAY   ☿ *Moon Age Day 19*   *Moon Sign Sagittarius*

If it is necessary to make small alterations to your routine, don't allow this to upset you. These are likely to have come about as a result of changing family requirements, together with a possible restlessness on the part of your partner. Just go with the flow and enjoy what comes along today, no matter whether it was your choice or not.

16 SUNDAY   ☿ *Moon Age Day 20*   *Moon Sign Sagittarius*

This should be one of the best days of the month as far as general progress is concerned and the only stumbling block could be that these trends come along on a Sunday. Expect a little resultant frustration and annoyance with the fact that the day does not contain the number of opportunities you might wish and you simply can't run the entire show.

17 MONDAY   ☿ *Moon Age Day 21*   *Moon Sign Capricorn*

This is an ideal time to be concentrating on securing a firmer financial footing and for strengthening your sense of security. You will have an advantage at present when it comes to attracting more cash and you have what it takes to plan effectively. New personalities are likely to be entering your life at any time this week.

18 TUESDAY   ☿ *Moon Age Day 22*   *Moon Sign Capricorn*

It appears that you now need to experiment all the time. That's fine because it is part of what makes you wiser but you may need to be careful that other people don't feel you are manipulating them to your own ends. As long as you remain sensitive to those around you this shouldn't happen and you can proceed as you wish.

19 WEDNESDAY   ☿ *Moon Age Day 23*   *Moon Sign Capricorn*

A diversity of interests would suit you best around the midweek period and you could easily become very bored if you only concentrate on the practical aspects of life. You need to allow your mind to wander a little and although you can't afford to take your eye off the ball in practical matters you can still enjoy some intellectual freedom.

20 THURSDAY ☿ *Moon Age Day 24 Moon Sign Aquarius*

Joint finances should be on the receiving end of a boost at any time now, even if you think that things are looking a bit gloomy on the money front. It's likely that there is something you have forgotten that can be used to your advantage or else you will soon find ways to draw on new resources and therefore feel more secure.

21 FRIDAY ☿ *Moon Age Day 25 Moon Sign Aquarius*

Look for ways to further advance your intellect today, and if you have been considering education of some kind, this could be an ideal time to put the wheels in motion. To others you look attractive, clever and dynamic but there are things within yourself that you still want to change. Even headstrong Aries should take things one at a time.

22 SATURDAY ☿ *Moon Age Day 26 Moon Sign Pisces*

You work very well at the moment with matters that require sorting and analysing. This is an ideal time for developing practical methods and routines and you will want to have everything in its place, especially at work. When it comes to your social life things could be rather more chaotic but generally speaking that's the way you like it.

23 SUNDAY ☿ *Moon Age Day 27 Moon Sign Pisces*

What you tend to look at right now is the big picture and life offers you new opportunities to get ahead. You won't be able to take up every offer that comes along otherwise you will crowd your schedule too much. The secret today lies in knowing which direction to take and which circumstances to leave well alone.

24 MONDAY ☿ *Moon Age Day 28 Moon Sign Pisces*

Not only do you want to learn more at the moment but you also have a tremendous capacity for seeing beyond the next horizon. Whilst others get lost in the details of life you push right through and achieve bigger and better objectives. You also have the capacity to expand your wisdom and your insight. Friends seek your advice today.

25 TUESDAY ☿ *Moon Age Day 0   Moon Sign Aries*

Things are likely to speed up noticeably now as the Moon races into your own zodiac sign. This is certainly not a day to rest on your laurels and if you act quickly you can make significant gains. Some of these are likely to be financial in nature but it has to be said that the very best trends during this lunar high are romantic.

26 WEDNESDAY ☿ *Moon Age Day 1   Moon Sign Aries*

You should be feeling at your very best now and will be dealing with what once looked like problems head on. In your present frame of mind there isn't much that is likely to get in your way and you have what it takes to impress most people. Put your luck to the test and be sure to recognise the green light when you see it.

27 THURSDAY ☿ *Moon Age Day 2   Moon Sign Taurus*

Today you can find ways to release the tremendous reservoir of energy that is bursting to get out of you. This is a good time to throw yourself fully into changes and alterations to your life that you know are going to be positive. You should also be energetic in your social life and will be doing things that others find terrifying.

28 FRIDAY ☿ *Moon Age Day 3   Moon Sign Taurus*

You can get ahead today as a result of the very real effort you are willing to put into everything you do. Money matters look more promising and you should also be getting on very well as far as your romantic life is concerned. By tomorrow things are likely to get better still, but even today there is no doubt you are on a roll.

29 SATURDAY ☿ *Moon Age Day 4   Moon Sign Gemini*

You will be very active today and anxious to learn anything that you sense is going to be of use to you in the future. This would be a very good time for educating yourself through travel or as a result of things you read. Not everyone agrees with your logic but in the end you have to make up your own mind.

30 SUNDAY ☿ *Moon Age Day 5 Moon Sign Gemini*

Discovering the lively and sparkling side of your personality is as easy as simply being yourself today. In almost all circumstances you shine like a star, a fact that those around you could hardly fail to notice. Your own self-esteem will be bolstered by the positive comments that come in from all those people who think you are great.

2017

May

1 MONDAY ☿ *Moon Age Day 6 Moon Sign Cancer*

Don't assume that everything you hear today is either accurate or truthful and maintain a degree of scepticism for maximum success. Of course you can trust those who are closest to you but as far as the wider world is concerned it does appear that there are people around now who would happily pull the wool over your eyes.

2 TUESDAY ☿ *Moon Age Day 7 Moon Sign Cancer*

Others seem more than ready to put themselves out on your behalf but as was the case yesterday you need to be just a little careful. If you rely on your excellent intuition you will automatically know who is trustworthy and who is not. In the best examples your friends seem willing to do almost anything to help you out.

3 WEDNESDAY ☿ *Moon Age Day 8 Moon Sign Leo*

Some developments can have unexpected but quite fortunate results at the moment, even though your approach to life today tends to be somewhat quieter and more contemplative than usual. You probably won't feel any urge to rush and because of this you are likely to make a much better job of some of the tasks you have to undertake.

4 THURSDAY *Moon Age Day 9 Moon Sign Leo*

There is a significant need for emotional fulfilment now and you are likely to analyse your most personal attachments to see how you can make them even better. Intimacy is indicated and you are much less inclined to plough all your energy into practical matters for a day or two. Aries is a great thinker just at the moment.

5 FRIDAY
Moon Age Day 10   Moon Sign Virgo

It seems as though the acquisition of money and possessions is likely to figure more strongly in your thinking today than has been the case for quite a while. You are looking for ways and means of making your life more comfortable and introducing to it a degree of leisure and luxury to which you would like to become accustomed.

6 SATURDAY
Moon Age Day 11   Moon Sign Virgo

The brighter the lights are at the moment the more you will enjoy life. At first glance this does not seem to be the best time for social interaction but you do need the cut and thrust that comes from being in the company of like-minded people. Be careful just now regarding your food and drink intake – especially the drink.

7 SUNDAY
Moon Age Day 12   Moon Sign Libra

This won't be the most dynamic day that you have ever experienced. The lunar low hangs around and brings you to a rather depressed or too-solid frame of mind. What you need the most is diversion and there are friends around who can bring you out of yourself if you only take the time out to give them the chance.

8 MONDAY
Moon Age Day 13   Moon Sign Libra

You could still be looking on the pessimistic side of life and certainly don't have what it takes to move mountains just at the moment. Fortunately there are some strong supporting planets in the background that make you ever anxious to look ahead and to plan for the short-term future. This does at least bring a welcome diversion.

9 TUESDAY
Moon Age Day 14   Moon Sign Libra

There is probably little or no privacy to be had at the moment as you throw in your lot with others and show a willingness to put your own momentary need for solitude on hold. You won't be retreating from any situation and show a definite need to interfere in just about anything. Friends may not altogether approve of your actions.

10 WEDNESDAY   *Moon Age Day 15   Moon Sign Scorpio*

If your love life isn't quite as satisfying as you would wish right now you can at least be sure that the answer to any problem lies in your own hands. Don't wait for others to make the first move but rather do what you can to sweep your partner off their feet. A few little gestures are probably all it takes to pep things up no end.

11 THURSDAY   *Moon Age Day 16   Moon Sign Scorpio*

This is certainly not the best day of the month to believe everything you hear, so bear this in mind if some news sounds strange and unlikely. Your reasoning is good and if ever there was a time to rely primarily on your own judgement, this is it. Your confidence grows and grows as the day wears on.

12 FRIDAY   *Moon Age Day 17   Moon Sign Sagittarius*

There is plenty of initiative about but a possibility that you tend to do and say the wrong things when it matters the most. Generally speaking these situations will be funny rather than important but Aries isn't always very good at laughing at itself. Don't be too precious today and accept the fact that life can be ludicrous sometimes.

13 SATURDAY   *Moon Age Day 18   Moon Sign Sagittarius*

There is a great deal to be said for friendship at the moment and you will probably be relying heavily on your pals, both inside and outside of work. It might be possible to arrange something very special for the sake of someone you care about a good deal and you may also be delving into relationships from the dim and distant past.

14 SUNDAY   *Moon Age Day 19   Moon Sign Sagittarius*

This can really be a Sunday to remember, though not because anything overtly sensational or exciting is happening. You have it within you now to find a deep sense of security and an overriding peace that sometimes eludes you. Look for interesting and historical places to go and spend precious moments with your partner.

15 MONDAY   *Moon Age Day 20   Moon Sign Capricorn*

Although on the one hand you might be exercising a little restraint from a fiscal point of view, you can also find ways and means to have a really good time today. That's because you are concentrating on aspects of life that don't cost you a penny. In particular you may well be in tune with gardens and growing things generally.

16 TUESDAY   *Moon Age Day 21   Moon Sign Capricorn*

Now you are very much on the ball and anxious to show just how much you know about a variety of subjects. All the same, you will do best today if you concentrate on those things at which you are an expert. Routines will seem something of a bore so stick to what interests you for today. Tomorrow is a better day for run-of-the-mill tasks.

17 WEDNESDAY   *Moon Age Day 22   Moon Sign Aquarius*

A few unexpected conflicts could put you on the wrong side of people you usually get along with very well. Avoid these by taking the time to talk things through and by admitting that there could be another point of view in addition to your own. The active and enterprising Aries subject will be very much on display today.

18 THURSDAY   *Moon Age Day 23   Moon Sign Aquarius*

This is one of the best times of the month for financial investments of almost any sort. You are level headed and unlikely to make rash decisions that you would come to regret later. At the same time you are now willing to take on sound advice and to admit that you can't be an expert in absolutely everything.

19 FRIDAY   *Moon Age Day 24   Moon Sign Pisces*

You attract people for intellectual reasons during this planetary interlude and you won't take kindly to individuals you consider to be either ignorant or lacking in intelligence. This is fine as far as it goes but you need to make sure that you don't come across as arrogant or overbearing.

20 SATURDAY   *Moon Age Day 25   Moon Sign Pisces*

Officials and people in positions of authority should prove to be quite agreeable at the moment – or is it that your attitude is so good that they can't fail to treat you well? In the end the reason isn't important. What is significant is that certain individuals you didn't have any time for in the past are now much easier to get on with.

21 SUNDAY   *Moon Age Day 26   Moon Sign Pisces*

Now you can make new friends and take an interest in new enterprises. You will be particularly interested in speculating about the future but as always with Aries it is the practical side of life that proves to be most rewarding. Contemplation is fine but Aries doesn't gain much from thoughts when there are actions to take.

22 MONDAY   *Moon Age Day 27   Moon Sign Aries*

The lunar high definitely brings out the best in you, not least because it offers all sorts of new starts and possibilities that are very welcome to Aries. With no shortage of things to occupy both your mind and your body this could be a day to remember. Only recalcitrant family members are likely to prove a little difficult.

23 TUESDAY   *Moon Age Day 28   Moon Sign Aries*

Rely heavily on your instincts at this stage of the week and be bold enough to follow your own convictions, no matter where they lead you. With extra energy and a great determination to do things the way you want it is very unlikely that you would meet much in the way of opposition under present planetary trends.

24 WEDNESDAY   *Moon Age Day 29   Moon Sign Taurus*

In many respects you are presently enjoying a period of significant stability, at least in terms of the way relationships are working out. Peace and quiet is something you ought to relish for today at least and you can take time out to enjoy the lengthening days and milder weather. An outdoor sort of day could suit you best of all.

25 THURSDAY
Moon Age Day 0   Moon Sign Taurus

Financial issues should continue to bring significant rewards and it appears that you are about as wise as you can be when it comes to practical matters. If there are any small problems in your family you ought to be able to sort these out by having a timely word here and there. You are very reasonable in your approach now.

26 FRIDAY
Moon Age Day 1   Moon Sign Gemini

Much of today is taken at a rapid pace and there won't always be time for those moments when you can offer reassurance to others. It may be necessary to set a little time aside in order to give the comfort and security that those around you crave, even if this comes at the expense of having to leave something until another day.

27 SATURDAY
Moon Age Day 2   Moon Sign Gemini

This is a time when you may get caught up in your own pursuits and you will be quite keen to spend at least some time on your own. Split the weekend as much as you can because there are also responsibilities that you cannot avoid. Family members are likely to be relying heavily on you for both advice and practical help.

28 SUNDAY
Moon Age Day 3   Moon Sign Cancer

There is plenty you can now do to feather your nest as far as your home life is concerned but when it comes to your career you will probably have to be patient for a day or two. Don't sit around wondering what you should do. This is most likely the one day of the week when you have the time to simply please yourself.

29 MONDAY
Moon Age Day 4   Moon Sign Cancer

This is a time of the month when you will be very creative and even inspirational in your thinking. If there is something at the back of your mind that has been troubling you for a while, now is the time to get it out into the open. Seize the chance for positive discussions both at home and at work.

30 TUESDAY   *Moon Age Day 5   Moon Sign Leo*

Matters may move ahead in your life much quicker than you might have expected so you will need to be right on the ball if you are going to make all the gains that are possible. Today is likely to be fast and furious in almost every way and your social nature is much stimulated by present planetary trends. Find ways to enjoy yourself.

31 WEDNESDAY   *Moon Age Day 6   Moon Sign Leo*

Now is the time to initiate sensible methods that will further your professional goals. Ideas that come into your head right now tend to be very practical in nature and you have the ability to follow these through. There isn't much in a planetary sense to throw a spanner in the works – unless of course you are too impulsive.

June

2017

1 THURSDAY
Moon Age Day 7   Moon Sign Virgo

It may surprise others today that you are so willing to give ground because you certainly don't show your usual desire to be in the driving seat. There's method in your madness because this reassures people that you understand that achievement does not come from applying undue pressure. Psychology works well for you now.

2 FRIDAY
Moon Age Day 8   Moon Sign Virgo

You may prefer your own company at the moment, though probably not for long. There are strongly vacillating tendencies about and the ability of others to understand your motivation remains in doubt. You need to explain yourself carefully and to be willing to address a different and sometimes radical point of view.

3 SATURDAY
Moon Age Day 9   Moon Sign Virgo

You are likely to be in a fairly insular mood and might opt to spend today getting on with practical jobs that have been waiting in the wings for some time. If you have difficulty understanding some issues, bear in mind that you might be looking over the top of some fairly fundamental truths.

4 SUNDAY
Moon Age Day 10   Moon Sign Libra

Your enthusiasm is inclined to flag somewhat today and you simply don't have enough energy to get on top of everything. Do your best to spread yourself about socially because the interaction you have with others will take your mind off small but significant concerns. Today might not be startling but can still be enjoyable.

5 MONDAY
Moon Age Day 11   Moon Sign Libra

A day when it would be ideal to take significant periods of rest but the necessities of life could make this more or less impossible. The way round this is to allow others to take some of the strain, whilst you decide to sit back and supervise. This is something Aries is quite good at doing and it is expected of you.

6 TUESDAY
Moon Age Day 12   Moon Sign Scorpio

This might not be the best day of all for using your logic and you will do far better if you employ your imagination and intuition at present. It's amazing what you can achieve by simply turning on the deeper qualities of your mind and by watching carefully the way others are behaving. Altogether a surprising day.

7 WEDNESDAY
Moon Age Day 13   Moon Sign Scorpio

Don't be too quick to jump to any conclusions today and wait until evidence comes in before you make up your mind about anything at all. This period might not turn out to be particularly exciting but it should be solid and can offer you a few unexpected gifts. Most of these are likely to be deeply personal in nature.

8 THURSDAY
Moon Age Day 14   Moon Sign Sagittarius

Avoid a tendency to be too much of a prima donna today because it doesn't really suit you and won't get you anywhere. People prefer you when you are your usual down-to-earth self and when you tell it how it is. Get some change into your life and especially into the lives of family members, some of whom are vegetating.

9 FRIDAY
Moon Age Day 15   Moon Sign Sagittarius

You now seem to have much more control over your own destiny and in particular the way things are going for you at work. Arians who are involved in full time education will probably work even harder than usual and will certainly be discovering that their understanding of certain matters is suddenly greater than before.

10 SATURDAY   *Moon Age Day 16   Moon Sign Sagittarius*

Co-operation and flexibility are the keywords under present planetary trends and you should find it possible to get on well with people who haven't always figured prominently in your life before. There are changes to be made to certain routines you normally take for granted but these should turn out to be for the best.

11 SUNDAY   *Moon Age Day 17   Moon Sign Capricorn*

Positive relationship highlights ought to be quite obvious today and you have exactly what it takes to get your own way in most situations. Not everyone will agree with your point of view but that doesn't really matter. The only slight problem might be the odd dent to your pride if others somehow modify your ideas.

12 MONDAY   *Moon Age Day 18   Moon Sign Capricorn*

You can hardly fail to make a positive impression today and you ought to feel generally very good about life and where you are going. The sheer force of your personality makes a great impression on just about everyone you encounter and you can rest assured that you are being talked about a great deal.

13 TUESDAY   *Moon Age Day 19   Moon Sign Aquarius*

What shows more clearly than anything today is your tremendous ability to bring out the best in others. This is true in almost any situation but is most emphasised if you take time out for leisure and pleasure pursuits. Any sort of major purchase made at this time could turn out to be a real bargain but you need to keep your eyes open.

14 WEDNESDAY   *Moon Age Day 20   Moon Sign Aquarius*

If you feel any sort of dissatisfaction at this stage of the working week it is likely to be because you are not allowed to follow a course of action that you know in your soul to be correct. Instead of kicking up a fuss about the situation simply wait and watch. Your moment will come, even if it's slightly further down the road.

15 THURSDAY   *Moon Age Day 21   Moon Sign Aquarius*

It is not what you do but what others think you are doing that really matters under present trends. For this reason you need to be sure to get your opinions across, leaving others in no doubt as to what you think. If people seem to be deliberately obtuse, it may simply be that they struggle to keep up with the pace of your ideas.

16 FRIDAY   *Moon Age Day 22   Moon Sign Pisces*

This is a good time to push for and realise financial benefits – perhaps even asking for a raise of salary. Of course you will want to choose your moment carefully and then show just how tactful you can be. This, together with proof positive that you are worth every penny, might mean that luck is on your side.

17 SATURDAY   *Moon Age Day 23   Moon Sign Pisces*

This is a period when you can definitely capitalise on important information. This is why it is so important to keep your ears open because you can't know in advance what is going to be significant and what isn't. With others you need to show how helpful you can be and to be on hand to sort out one or two muddles.

18 SUNDAY   *Moon Age Day 24   Moon Sign Aries*

A potentially lucky period comes along and with the lunar high predominating across the weekend and beyond this would be an excellent time for travel and for seeing new sights. Don't get tied down with routines or everyday matters and wherever possible ring the changes. Make sure there are good friends around to enjoy life with you.

19 MONDAY   *Moon Age Day 25   Moon Sign Aries*

A lucky streak remains in operation and you will still be anxious to cash in on this most fortuitous phase. With little time for rules and regulations it looks as though you want to do everything your own way and you certainly won't take no for an answer when you know you have the measure of just about any situation.

20 TUESDAY   *Moon Age Day 26   Moon Sign Taurus*

It's time to be making new investments, though not nearly all of these will have anything to do with money. Time is the greatest investment of all for Aries because you have so much to do with yours. Extra effort in terms of supporting friends and family members is likely to pay great dividends later.

21 WEDNESDAY   *Moon Age Day 27   Moon Sign Taurus*

Your potential for achieving professional goals remains essentially strong, though you might have to do more in order to convince people at home that you are concerned and committed. Any tendency to be casual over issues that others see as being very important won't win you any house points at all at this stage of the week.

22 THURSDAY   *Moon Age Day 28   Moon Sign Gemini*

There is much interest to be found now from social interests and you have what it takes to mix business and pleasure in a potentially rewarding way. Stay alert to new information because you cannot know in advance just how much you are likely to learn. An open attitude means all sorts of possibilities can come your way.

23 FRIDAY   *Moon Age Day 29   Moon Sign Gemini*

Your curiosity is now off the scale and your intellectual powers are especially well honed. There isn't much that will pass you by and you are able to notice the little nuances of life that can make all the difference. There are some interesting people around at this time of the month and you ought to be particularly competent at work.

24 SATURDAY   *Moon Age Day 0   Moon Sign Cancer*

You may be able to make financial gains via speculations of one sort or another. Although it would not be sensible to put your shirt on the next horse running, you will be shrewd and discriminating enough to know when you can chance your arm a little. Some extra tact may be required in discussions with family members or friends.

25 SUNDAY
Moon Age Day 1   Moon Sign Cancer

The Sun is now in your solar fourth house and it is important across the next month or so that you set aside a little time to be with people you care for deeply. There are likely to be changes taking place in and around your home and you will be expected to take part and to offer sensible opinions on quite a few occasions.

26 MONDAY
Moon Age Day 2   Moon Sign Leo

A domestic or family matter is on your mind and no matter how you try you can't get away from it. It may not have occurred to you but the best way forward would be to sort the situation out. This might require a fairly serious heart-to-heart, though do bear in mind that your approach can sometimes be rather too brusque for some people.

27 TUESDAY
Moon Age Day 3   Moon Sign Leo

There could be rewards on the home front around this time and younger people in particular will find ways to delight you. It's likely that you will be doing all you can to support your relatives, whilst at the same time keeping an eye on a particular friend who is having difficulties. Stresses and strains are evident but you deal with them.

28 WEDNESDAY
Moon Age Day 4   Moon Sign Leo

Perhaps you will prefer a range of interests today and if so you will need to turn your imagination up to full. Look forward to an influx of new ideas and listen to what your friends have to offer. Co-operation can be the key to social success and at the same time you have your most romantic head on at this time.

29 THURSDAY
Moon Age Day 5   Moon Sign Virgo

You must learn patience and this is the one lesson that is very difficult for Aries subjects. At the moment you can't have everything you would wish and a little prior planning is extremely important. Keeping your nerve in a tight situation at some time today is far less of a problem to you, as a zodiac sign that is naturally courageous.

30 FRIDAY
Moon Age Day 6   Moon Sign Virgo

The art of good conversation is part of what makes today special, or potentially so, for the average Aries person. You are on good terms with almost everyone and can actually score points with people you haven't especially cared for in the past. A cultured end to the day would be good – so how about a concert or a play?

2017

1 SATURDAY
Moon Age Day 7   Moon Sign Libra

It could seem as if life is a struggle for the moment but you are hardly in a good position to judge whilst the lunar low is around. Take this weekend steadily and find ways to enjoy yourself, freed from some of the restrictions that life seems to have placed upon you of late. The whole picture will soon look very different.

2 SUNDAY
Moon Age Day 8   Moon Sign Libra

This is a day during which you will probably be very happy to sit back and take stock of situations – without acting or interfering in things too much. Your mind can wander anywhere you wish and you may also have the chance to get away from everyday routines altogether. Keep an open mind about suggested changes.

3 MONDAY
Moon Age Day 9   Moon Sign Scorpio

You remain as happy as you always are when you can do something for another person but just at the moment you will have to concentrate a little more on what you can do for yourself. This is not a case of being selfish because only when you have your own life sorted the way you want can you really be of use to others.

4 TUESDAY
Moon Age Day 10   Moon Sign Scorpio

Whilst it looks as though you may be making progress at work, there is just a slight possibility that relationships with colleagues might be slightly strained for some reason. This is a situation you can address because it could be as simple as a misunderstanding that goes back days or even weeks.

5 WEDNESDAY *Moon Age Day 11   Moon Sign Scorpio*

A slight but important boost to your ego could well come along today. What form it will take is in some doubt but the most likely eventuality is that others will single you out for special attention and praise. Although you will shrug off the compliments they will be quite important to you.

6 THURSDAY *Moon Age Day 12   Moon Sign Sagittarius*

Some issues might now prove to be rather more trouble than they are worth and as a result a high degree of patience is going to be necessary. Extra care is essential when you are dealing with colleagues, some of whom might not appear to know what is expected of them. Explain situations two or three times if you have to.

7 FRIDAY *Moon Age Day 13   Moon Sign Sagittarius*

Look out for new ways to make money and for different approaches to old issues. Your mind is now working overtime and it is only a matter of hours before you will be putting new plans into action. A little patience is still necessary when dealing with friends or colleagues because some of them seem to have lost the plot.

8 SATURDAY *Moon Age Day 14   Moon Sign Capricorn*

Extended negotiations and major decisions make today somewhat trying but nevertheless extremely worthwhile. There is likely to be new information coming your way at the moment and you really do need to keep your ears and eyes open if you are to make the most of what is on offer from a number of different directions.

9 SUNDAY *Moon Age Day 15   Moon Sign Capricorn*

This ought to be a time during which family matters go extremely well. That's got to be good on a Sunday and there are likely to be offers around that will take you out of yourself completely. If you happen to work today you need to show extra care because it looks as though you are not taking account of the finer details.

10 MONDAY   *Moon Age Day 16   Moon Sign Capricorn*

Although the start of a new working week might seem to offer more of the same, you ought to now be sensing that things generally are about to change. Below the surface there is a sort of fountain of enthusiasm bubbling up inside you and despite the fact that there are some real frustrations around now, you are aware they won't last.

11 TUESDAY   *Moon Age Day 17   Moon Sign Aquarius*

It is clear that you now want to be on the move and there are likely to be very few circumstances that will work against your best interests. Don't sit around at home today, even if those around you seem less than willing to do anything. It's better to do things on your own at present than to feel you are vegetating in any way.

12 WEDNESDAY   *Moon Age Day 18   Moon Sign Aquarius*

There is great energy and drive around now – so much so that it might be difficult to know exactly what you are going to tackle next. The fact is that you want to get everything done at once and this could prove to be a slight problem. Bear in mind that it should be possible to delegate and to let others deal with the routines.

13 THURSDAY   *Moon Age Day 19   Moon Sign Pisces*

You have a strong tendency today towards intellectual pursuits of one sort or another and it is clear that you intend to test yourself as much as possible. Pitting your wits against friends and colleagues it appears that you will prove something to yourself about just how deep your intelligence runs. These exercises feed you with confidence.

14 FRIDAY   *Moon Age Day 20   Moon Sign Pisces*

Success comes at the moment from being properly organised but at the same time you should take care not to let new opportunities pass you by. Although you may not be in quite the right frame of mind to be starting new adventures you should at least register your interest so that people know you are anxious to participate.

15 SATURDAY   *Moon Age Day 21   Moon Sign Aries*

There is nothing remotely slow or steady about your life at the moment and if there is any problem at all it might be that you don't have the chance to enjoy some of your successes. All the same there is likely to be a real sense of achievement about at present, made even more enjoyable by the attention you get from other people.

16 SUNDAY   *Moon Age Day 22   Moon Sign Aries*

There is an ongoing confidence obvious in almost everything you do, which is added to by the attention coming in at you from the world outside. Even strangers seem to recognise your capabilities and it is a fact that almost everyone you meet is anxious to know you better. This is the time of times for Aries and a period to be relished.

17 MONDAY   *Moon Age Day 23   Moon Sign Aries*

It is possible that you will now find yourself in the company of a new friend or social contacts that haven't shown themselves before. Make the most of chance meetings and unusual happenings to register your own progress in life and also find the necessary time to prove to your partner or sweetheart how important they are.

18 TUESDAY   *Moon Age Day 24   Moon Sign Taurus*

Your intuition plays a greater part in your life at the moment and when something just doesn't seem to be the way it appears you should stop and take note. You can do yourself all sorts of favours right now by simply being in the right place at the right time to act. There is a much more decisive quality about you from today on.

19 WEDNESDAY   *Moon Age Day 25   Moon Sign Taurus*

Your attitude grows more expansive and you are now likely to be trying new things simply for the sake of seeing what the results might be. You are very experimental in your approach to life and will want to know how and why everything is the way it is. Others may laugh at you but that won't bother you at all.

20 THURSDAY *Moon Age Day 26   Moon Sign Gemini*

Being ambitious and hard working comes quite naturally to Aries and although you might be feeling slightly detached and withdrawn, that's not how things appear to those who watch you. To them you are go-getting and ambitious. Colleagues should be doubly helpful today and you find yourself mixing business with pleasure.

21 FRIDAY *Moon Age Day 27   Moon Sign Gemini*

One of your greatest gifts is your ability to motivate others. This is much emphasised at the moment and you can get the very best out of family members and friends but especially your life partner. You should also feel yourself to be slightly luckier than of late and as a result will probably find ways to indulge in a little speculation.

22 SATURDAY *Moon Age Day 28   Moon Sign Cancer*

You enjoy being out in front and very personable. Whatever opportunities come your way you will be inclined to jump on them immediately and to take advantage of the good nature and help of those around you. At home you show yourself to be warm and caring – which is why so much love is coming back in your direction.

23 SUNDAY *Moon Age Day 0   Moon Sign Cancer*

Those Aries people who have chosen this time to take a holiday will be the luckiest of all but even if this is not you, you ought to be able to arrange short outings. You may feel a strong desire to get out and see the world and simply flicking through the pages of travel brochures is hardly likely to be enough.

24 MONDAY *Moon Age Day 1   Moon Sign Leo*

Talking and listening come in equal measure today and you should be able to move forward in terms of your own plans to a much greater extent than seems to have been the case during the last few weeks. The start of this particular working week may coincide with good news on the professional front and also with revitalised romance.

25 TUESDAY   *Moon Age Day 2   Moon Sign Leo*

Social issues look settled and happy, leaving you with more time and greater incentive to make new friends and to avoid any sort of unpleasantness in your dealings with others. You are confident, and can be trusted to do the right thing under almost all circumstances – though do be wary of get-rich-quick schemes.

26 WEDNESDAY   *Moon Age Day 3   Moon Sign Virgo*

The emphasis tends to be much more on fun and self-expression right now than it will be on responsibility. Let others take the strain whilst you have fun with people you are happy to be around. You now need wide-open spaces and plenty of fresh air in order to feed your zest for life in the best way that proves to be possible.

27 THURSDAY   *Moon Age Day 4   Moon Sign Virgo*

Your thinking today is basically practical, with a veneer of common sense that will protect you against trying too hard in the wrong direction. You also have good intuition, a factor that will stand you in good stead when you have to deal with dubious types or situations with which you are unfamiliar.

28 FRIDAY   *Moon Age Day 5   Moon Sign Libra*

This should prove to be an industrious time and one during which the forces of life are flowing your way. The end of the working week could bring some pleasant surprises and you will be delightful to know. After a month during which circumstances sometimes held you back they are now much more likely to go your way.

29 SATURDAY   *Moon Age Day 6   Moon Sign Libra*

This won't be the best day of the month for many Arians, but neither is it likely to be as potent or difficult as the lunar low sometimes turns out to be. Keep it quiet and steady for today and tomorrow – doing those things that feed your intellect more than your pocket. This is a thinking time and a very potent one if you are careful.

30 SUNDAY
Moon Age Day 7   Moon Sign Libra

It may feel as if there are just too many responsibilities bearing down on you at present but this is a very temporary interlude and by the end of the weekend quite a few more answers should be coming your way. In particular, avoid worrying about family matters because some situations are storms in a teacup.

31 MONDAY
Moon Age Day 8   Moon Sign Scorpio

Look out for opportunities that allow you to enjoy yourself in specific ways. These probably don't include staying too close to home. It would be good to spend time in the company of people who stimulate the more intellectual side of your nature, maybe by visiting historical or cultural centres of one sort or another.

August

2017

1 TUESDAY
Moon Age Day 9   Moon Sign Scorpio

Your current ability to focus all the energy you presently feel is the reason why you should be getting on so well. With a tremendous sense of freedom surrounding you it is also likely again that you will take any opportunity to travel. Most experiences tend to be positive ones and you are just bursting to talk all day.

2 WEDNESDAY
Moon Age Day 10   Moon Sign Sagittarius

This is another great day for getting involved and for being the natural leader that your star-sign shows you to be. Although you will be involved in group activities there isn't much doubt that others see you as being in command and that means you can have things very much your own way. Cash should be easier to come by, too.

3 THURSDAY
Moon Age Day 11   Moon Sign Sagittarius

You are likely to throw a great deal of energy into your work today and there won't be all that much time for personal enjoyment. This is mainly because you are insistent on getting as much as possible done at this stage of the week. Although you can achieve a lot today it might be better to pace yourself just a little.

4 FRIDAY
Moon Age Day 12   Moon Sign Sagittarius

Home and family are under the planetary spotlight today as you find yourself making gains in all areas of life that are personal and even private. The deeper side of your nature is definitely in evidence but this won't prevent you from continuing to enjoy yourself – it's just that now you are doing so in quite different ways from usual.

5 SATURDAY   *Moon Age Day 13   Moon Sign Capricorn*

You are now in a period when it ought to be very easy to gather the information you need in order to get on better in a general sense. Your curiosity is roused and you will leave nothing to chance. Because you have so much energy even the most insignificant details fall under your scrutiny and that means greater advancement.

6 SUNDAY   *Moon Age Day 14   Moon Sign Capricorn*

There are fresh ideas about and a great desire to push the bounds of the possible in any way you can. Today marks one of those periods when you could feel slightly tied down by convention and you will be determined to get away somehow. This could mean a holiday but even a day or two away from routines would be welcome.

7 MONDAY   *Moon Age Day 15   Moon Sign Aquarius*

When it comes to achieving your objectives today couldn't really be better. At work you show yourself to be more than capable of coming up with new ideas and there is a strong chance that some sort of advancement will be coming your way. At the very least your versatility is being noticed and that stands you in good stead generally.

8 TUESDAY   *Moon Age Day 16   Moon Sign Aquarius*

Your career now seems to be boosted by a really intense period of concentration – together with the ability to put plans into practice that might not have seemed possible before. Stretching the bounds of the credible is what Aries is all about at the best of times but this skill is more finely tuned than ever under present trends.

9 WEDNESDAY   *Moon Age Day 17   Moon Sign Pisces*

Although your workload could seem rather heavy, you undertake almost everything with a smile on your face and a tune in your voice. This fact is clearly noticed by others and you should find that your influence with the world at large is greater than ever. This is achieved by simply being the person you naturally are.

10 THURSDAY   *Moon Age Day 18   Moon Sign Pisces*

There are many light-hearted times to be had in a social sense, with new friends to be made and a consolidation of the affection you feel for people who are always around you. If you don't feel contented at the moment you may not be trying hard enough, though it has to be said that Aries is always searching and perpetually on the move.

11 FRIDAY   *Moon Age Day 19   Moon Sign Pisces*

It is towards the practical aspects of life that your mind is now inclined to turn – though you may be working harder than ever to impress someone you find attractive. In return the attention you get from others is noteworthy, even to the extent that people are positively queuing up to do you all the favours they can.

12 SATURDAY   *Moon Age Day 20   Moon Sign Aries*

Your sense of direction is absolutely clear at the moment and you are unfettered by pointless worries about possible consequences. It might even be suggested that you are very calculating under the influence of the lunar high but this is no problem either, particularly since you are working towards the success of others as well as yourself.

13 SUNDAY   ☿   *Moon Age Day 21   Moon Sign Aries*

Good things are definitely likely to be happening to you today and you can enjoy this part of August in the knowledge that most of what you want is going your way. With more than your fair share of good luck it looks as though you will be quite happy to take a few chances – though of a financial rather than a personal nature.

14 MONDAY   ☿   *Moon Age Day 22   Moon Sign Taurus*

It's a fact that there are times when the sign of Aries needs a little intellectual refreshment and such a period might be upon you now. In all probability you will insist on clearing up certain priorities before you get round to thinking about enjoyment but this is August after all – a month that was designed for fun and particularly so for you.

15 TUESDAY ☿ *Moon Age Day 23 Moon Sign Taurus*

This is just the right time of the year to express the lighter side of your nature and to be as entertaining as Aries at its best can be. Getting together with like-minded individuals is what is important during this period and you will be especially attracted now to other people from your own part of the zodiac.

16 WEDNESDAY ☿ *Moon Age Day 24 Moon Sign Gemini*

Meeting new people is what keeps you stimulated at the moment and you should also be in a very good position to make greater headway in your work. Seek out like-minded people and swap ideas with them. They say great minds think alike and although this is broadly true it can also said that difference breeds success.

17 THURSDAY ☿ *Moon Age Day 25 Moon Sign Gemini*

You tend to be successful in business matters this week and your mind will be very ordered. Having to deal with a few awkward types could hold you back a little today, but in the main you will brush problems aside easily. This might not be so easy in matters associated with romance because here diplomacy and tact are necessary.

18 FRIDAY ☿ *Moon Age Day 26 Moon Sign Cancer*

You are now prone to touchiness in your dealings with the world at large and since this is so unlike you it is likely to come as a shock to some of the people around you. You can blame present planetary trends for this tendency but there are some strong supporting planets around too and these offer you a calmer influence.

19 SATURDAY ☿ *Moon Age Day 27 Moon Sign Cancer*

There ought to be a great deal going on in your social life but nothing is going to be more important to you today than showing your love and regard for that someone special in your life. Friendships shine out strongly and you could find yourself back in the warm embrace of someone who had previously disappeared from your life.

20 SUNDAY   ☿   *Moon Age Day 28*   *Moon Sign Leo*

You will definitely feel the need to be on top now and it would take someone very competent and extremely clever to get ahead of you in the power-stakes. Despite your feelings of dominance, you still show a strong desire to help those around you – but of course you will want them to show how very grateful they are in return!

21 MONDAY   ☿   *Moon Age Day 29*   *Moon Sign Leo*

In your dealings with colleagues you need to stick to the point so that there is no chance of misinterpretation or confusion. Give yourself a small pat on the back regarding something that has gone your way recently but don't get so caught up with congratulations that you take your eye off the ball. There are opponents about.

22 TUESDAY   ☿   *Moon Age Day 0*   *Moon Sign Virgo*

If you find that you are unsure regarding a specific plan of action it might help if you enlist the support of people who are really in the know. The same is generally true when it comes to jobs that need doing around the house. It will probably prove to be cheaper and easier to get someone in than to struggle with them yourself.

23 WEDNESDAY ☿   *Moon Age Day 1*   *Moon Sign Virgo*

You have an inventive, quick mind that tends to race ahead of others in almost all situations. That's fine except for the fact that sometimes people don't understand your actions or even the reasoning behind them. It would help today if you were willing to explain yourself and even to spell things out in very specific terms.

24 THURSDAY   ☿   *Moon Age Day 2*   *Moon Sign Virgo*

You show yourself to be both spontaneous and fascinating to know and will be doing all you can to make those around you as happy as possible. Nothing will appeal to you more now than the prospect of getting out and about with individuals who feed your intellect and who seem to think about things just as you do.

25 FRIDAY ☿ *Moon Age Day 3   Moon Sign Libra*

It is just possible that your expectations are going to be too high for the next two or three days. The lunar low comes as the first stumbling block since the Sun moved into Libra and you need to be just a little wary of doing more than is strictly necessary. Your love life should be good at present with plenty of romantic attention on the way.

26 SATURDAY ☿ *Moon Age Day 4   Moon Sign Libra*

This is not a good time for business initiatives but is an excellent period for enjoying what your home life and personal attachments have to offer, which is handy at the weekend. Don't try to achieve too much. It won't do you any harm at all to stick fast for a while, though nothing will prevent your mind from being progressive.

27 SUNDAY ☿ *Moon Age Day 5   Moon Sign Scorpio*

It won't be possible to get on equally well with everyone today but that is as much due to their attitudes as it is to your own. Stay away from those you find vexatious or who wind you up unnecessarily. It would be far better today to spend as much time as you can in the company of people you have known for a very long time.

28 MONDAY ☿ *Moon Age Day 6   Moon Sign Scorpio*

Social settings are the best ones to be in today, even though you may be putting most of your effort into your work. It seems that you get on better when you are not really trying and there may be an object lesson here. There is a distinct possibility that you are trying too hard in some spheres of your life. Relax and enjoy the ride.

29 TUESDAY ☿ *Moon Age Day 7   Moon Sign Sagittarius*

You may now wish to break from your normal routines and could so easily be getting restless as September beckons. There is great potential for travel, even if you hadn't really thought about doing so at this time. Certain people are relying on you heavily and you won't be doing anything to let them down. Your partner may need some advice.

126

30 WEDNESDAY ☿ *Moon Age Day 8   Moon Sign Sagittarius*

You want even more freedom of self-expression and will take any opportunity to tell others what you think. Your opinions might not always be welcome but in the main you retain your popularity and will be high in the esteem of those around you. This is a day that will work best if you find something new and different to do.

31 THURSDAY ☿ *Moon Age Day 9   Moon Sign Sagittarius*

Today marks an easier-going phase and you should find everything running in a very smooth way. Where money is concerned you could be rather better off than you expected to be and there are new opportunities coming along all the time. Take advantage of the co-operative tendencies of family members.

September

2017

1 FRIDAY
☿ *Moon Age Day 10   Moon Sign Capricorn*

A boost to your finances could crop up now, or at the very least you should notice that things are looking better for the short-term future. Although a good deal of your time is now spent planning ahead there are situations around today that demand your immediate attention and some quick thinking will pay significant dividends.

2 SATURDAY
☿ *Moon Age Day 11   Moon Sign Capricorn*

Your mind is now working very quickly and you are acutely aware of the motivations of both colleagues and friends. These insights are deep and profound, so much so that you will be in a position to help people out of a dilemma even before they realise there is any problem. Some people might think you are 'weird' but they will be grateful.

3 SUNDAY
☿ *Moon Age Day 12   Moon Sign Aquarius*

This may be one of the best days of September when it comes to making money – or for getting notification that your ideas from the past are now beginning to bear fruit. Some jobs could seem endless but it won't take you long to get where you want to be in a general sense and a little extra effort now will prove really worthwhile.

4 MONDAY
☿ *Moon Age Day 13   Moon Sign Aquarius*

There could be considerable gains to be made at the moment but if you really want to cash in it's a case of keeping your finger on the financial pulse all the time. This might get a bit tedious because although Aries people love the results of money they are not the most patient people in the world and you need variety.

5 TUESDAY ☿ *Moon Age Day 14   Moon Sign Aquarius*

Today you will feel right at home in a world of concepts and you can grasp the bigger picture with very little information. Not everyone will be able to keep up with your lightning-quick reasoning and there will be times when it is necessary to either slow down or else to push ahead on your own. Routines will seem very boring at present.

6 WEDNESDAY ☿ *Moon Age Day 15   Moon Sign Pisces*

Today is especially favourable for close partnerships. These could be of a romantic nature but you are just as likely to find yourself growing ever closer to a colleague or to someone who was until recently nothing more than an acquaintance. You appear to have plenty to keep you busy but find time to monitor the bigger picture.

7 THURSDAY ☿ *Moon Age Day 16   Moon Sign Pisces*

There ought to be plenty of opportunities for you to get ahead today and you can make great headway in your career. If you are involved in education at the moment you can expect to be grasping the nettle firmly and will probably come to a good understanding of something that has eluded you up to now.

8 FRIDAY ☿ *Moon Age Day 17   Moon Sign Aries*

Things change dramatically with the arrival of the lunar high and you certainly won't be hanging in the background now. On the contrary you want to be where the action is and will take almost any calculated risk in order to steal a march on colleagues. Like a surfer, once you get on the wave today you want to ride it all the way.

9 SATURDAY ☿ *Moon Age Day 18   Moon Sign Aries*

Here and now is all that matters to you at present and this may be the best chance you get during the whole of September to make the best impression. Look out for people you don't see very often and make them important in your life again. Your powers of persuasion are now second-to-none and you exude confidence.

10 SUNDAY ☿ *Moon Age Day 19   Moon Sign Taurus*

Some deep thinking and even soul-searching is on the cards and you may well spend a good deal of time today looking back to incidents from the past. This is fine just as long as you are using them as a yardstick for your behaviour in the future but do remember that for Aries especially there isn't really any future in the past.

11 MONDAY ☿ *Moon Age Day 20   Moon Sign Taurus*

Money matters should be at the forefront of your thinking and this would be an ideal time during which to start a new business or to get involved in some form of interesting but safe speculation. You appear to be thinking well ahead and have what it takes to be of great use to family members, colleagues and friends.

12 TUESDAY ☿ *Moon Age Day 21   Moon Sign Gemini*

Your mind is in a hurry, and probably also something of a turmoil, which could lead to problems if you don't slow things down. Make a very definite effort to be steady in your approach to life generally. This is particularly important when you are dealing with people you don't know very well. Act only when you are sure of yourself.

13 WEDNESDAY *Moon Age Day 22   Moon Sign Gemini*

Harmony and peaceful coexistence might not be an option today. Although you want to get on well with everyone, certain people may not be giving you that option. Don't start arguments but if they come your way you will want to win them quickly and efficiently. Now is the time to tell it how it is.

14 THURSDAY *Moon Age Day 23   Moon Sign Cancer*

You will be at your best today when you are amongst close friends and people you trust a great deal. It would be sensible at the moment to make a special fuss of your partner. Even though there may be no anniversary or special event to celebrate you should buy your lover a gift or do something to sweep them off their feet.

15 FRIDAY *Moon Age Day 24   Moon Sign Cancer*

This can be a great time for creative self-expression. Others will value your opinions and will be actively turning to you for the sort of advice you alone can offer. There is a strong recognition that you are somehow 'in the know' and even people living at a distance could be ringing or emailing you to pick your brains.

16 SATURDAY *Moon Age Day 25   Moon Sign Cancer*

Today you will be able to deal positively with a past issue and also put your personal life into a better focus. Maybe there have been arguments around and you will want to do everything you can to put an end to these. Nevertheless yours is a very reactive zodiac sign and you can't expect to agree with everyone all of the time.

17 SUNDAY *Moon Age Day 26   Moon Sign Leo*

Do what you can to stimulate new and fascinating attachments but at the same time make sure that these don't interfere with your most intimate relationships. It is just possible under present trends that you could be inspiring a little jealousy in your partner and though this is without justification it may be understandable.

18 MONDAY *Moon Age Day 27   Moon Sign Leo*

Generally speaking this ought to be a great time for wheeling and dealing. Do all the business you can this week and capitalise on the good circumstances that surround you on all sides. It's time to get busy and there should be plenty of people in your vicinity who will be more than happy to throw in their lot with you.

19 TUESDAY *Moon Age Day 28   Moon Sign Virgo*

Your mind is still sharp and you are excellent at letting others know what everyone ought to be doing. Don't be too surprised, though, if someone has ideas of their own and refuses to follow your advice. As a result your perfect model of life can be shattered at a stroke – though not of course if you remain flexible and open-minded.

20 WEDNESDAY   *Moon Age Day 0   Moon Sign Virgo*

It would be wise to listen to the advice of people in your vicinity today – especially those for whom you have the greatest respect. Make sure that you have all the relevant information before you decide on a plan of action. This is a period when it would be best to gather together all the information you can.

21 THURSDAY   *Moon Age Day 1   Moon Sign Libra*

Take stock of your affairs and by all means plan ahead but don't try to get too much done in a concrete sense. The general level of luck that often attends your life is not likely to be present at the moment and this certainly is not the right time of the month for any form of speculation or for taking on excessive challenges.

22 FRIDAY   *Moon Age Day 2   Moon Sign Libra*

It would be all too easy today to strain or sprain something – so when it comes to exercise of any sort take it steady. Actually your nature is such at the moment that you probably will not want to push yourself and Aries would be far happier right now lazing around and allowing others to do most of the hard work.

23 SATURDAY   *Moon Age Day 3   Moon Sign Scorpio*

There are a few trends around at the moment that will incline you to look back rather than forward. Aries is going through a nostalgic phase and it is likely that elements of your past will replay in your mind a great deal in the days ahead. In itself this isn't a problem as long as you remember that for Aries things can only 'happen' in the present.

24 SUNDAY   *Moon Age Day 4   Moon Sign Scorpio*

A strong boost to finances is indicated – that is if you put yourself in the best position to benefit from these positive trends. This will mean keeping your eyes open and also relies on you acting quickly when you know the time is right. New and valuable information is there for the taking so make sure you don't ignore it.

25 MONDAY   *Moon Age Day 5   Moon Sign Scorpio*

Love life and romantic matters generally are likely to be going your way today. You will be slightly less contentious and probably choosing a version of the truth that others find easier to stomach. You engage others rather than dominating them and that's all it takes to persuade them to do things your way.

26 TUESDAY   *Moon Age Day 6   Moon Sign Sagittarius*

Certain matters in your personal life could be either misleading or confused today and it would be worth talking things through carefully in order to discover what is really going on. A little care may be necessary if you hit a few setbacks, especially when you are trying to understand what makes younger family members tick.

27 WEDNESDAY   *Moon Age Day 7   Moon Sign Sagittarius*

There could be minor tensions about today and though individually these mean little, when lumped together frustration is likely to be the result. Withdraw somewhat from the rat race and spend a few hours on your own. If this isn't possible during the day it ought to be more likely in the evening. It's hard to fall out with yourself!

28 THURSDAY   *Moon Age Day 8   Moon Sign Capricorn*

Things are on the up again and what looked confusing or problematic yesterday now comes into sharp relief. Once you identify potential stumbling blocks you are well able to deal with them and as a result the path before you looks less strewn with rocks. Your usual cheerful nature will also be a distinct advantage in social settings today.

29 FRIDAY   *Moon Age Day 9   Moon Sign Capricorn*

Your interests may now turn towards cultural matters and there is great interest about when it comes to mixing with people or associations that have not played a part in your life up to now. You will also be very charity-minded and will find ways to help out those who you see as being far less fortunate than yourself.

30 SATURDAY   *Moon Age Day 10   Moon Sign Capricorn*

You will need to be quite disciplined this weekend if you want to get the very best of what is on offer. There is just a slight tendency for you to let certain things slide, or to expect others to take up the slack. There are some decisions that only you can make and if you do leave them to those around you the results could be chaotic.

October

2017

1 SUNDAY
Moon Age Day 11   Moon Sign Aquarius

You may find that you need to adapt if you want to get the very best out of life at the moment. For the last few days you have been under the influence of a few slightly awkward planetary influences and these could have left you feeling somewhat muddled. Today offers you the chance to think things through and to take action.

2 MONDAY
Moon Age Day 12   Moon Sign Aquarius

There could be a few troublesome domestic issues to be sorted out at the start of this week and that might lead to you getting behind in other matters. Exercise all the patience you can and simply do what seems necessary. You can catch up later and in any case it is a matter of priorities in the end.

3 TUESDAY
Moon Age Day 13   Moon Sign Pisces

Don't be bossy at home and allow family members to choose options for themselves. You don't mean to interfere, it's just your way, but others may not appreciate your seeming to know better than they do how to run their lives. If you listen and comment but avoid interference you can still have an input.

4 WEDNESDAY
Moon Age Day 14   Moon Sign Pisces

This could be one of the best times of the month for involving yourself in community issues and for getting to grips with a slight problem that has a bearing on just about everyone you know. You are very socially minded at the moment and the reforming tendencies of Aries show out strongly. You might even be quite political.

5 THURSDAY
Moon Age Day 15   Moon Sign Aries

Stand by for an explosion of possibilities and do everything you can to meet this very progressive period in a reactive way. The lunar high should bring better general luck, together with a fund of new incentives and plenty of energy to pursue them. All in all this could be the most influential day that you will encounter during October.

6 FRIDAY
Moon Age Day 16   Moon Sign Aries

This is the best time of the month to be running ahead of the pack. So quick are your thought processes that it is unlikely many people will be able to keep up with you. The new incentives continue and at the same time you have what it takes to sweep someone right off their feet. As a result new romance is possible for some.

7 SATURDAY
Moon Age Day 17   Moon Sign Taurus

Don't allow the views of others to influence your judgements to such an extent that you fail to address issues yourself. Aries might be just a little lazy at the moment and for that reason alone it will be easier to simply go with the flow. Force yourself to think about matters yourself and take whatever actions your mind suggests.

8 SUNDAY
Moon Age Day 18   Moon Sign Taurus

You need to keep moving and to follow up all possibilities as and when they arise. There won't be too much time to spend with loved ones but even a few words of reassurance might be all it takes to keep things sweet at home. Meanwhile you will be going wherever the action is and should stay well in charge of your own destiny.

9 MONDAY
Moon Age Day 19   Moon Sign Taurus

You enjoy a good balance of give and take right now and should find certain individuals to be far more giving than might have been the case only a few days ago. With plenty of determination you won't be easily beaten but there might be one particular issue that despite all your efforts should now be reluctantly abandoned.

10 TUESDAY
Moon Age Day 20   Moon Sign Gemini

Organisational issues take up a good deal of your time at the moment. This could be related to work but is just as likely to be concerned with social issues and your need to ring the changes in terms of out-of-work interests. Keep in touch with friends who are at a distance and maybe arrange a long journey to be taken next year.

11 WEDNESDAY
Moon Age Day 21   Moon Sign Gemini

Don't allow yourself to be manipulated by others but instead look at all situations yourself and react according to your own conscience. Aries is a natural leader and not a follower, which is why in the end you may bring others round to your own point of view. It's a fine line, though, because bullying certainly won't work at present.

12 THURSDAY
Moon Age Day 22   Moon Sign Cancer

Life can be somewhat trying in some ways and yet very positive in others – it's simply a matter of choosing your path carefully for the moment. Although you may be on the receiving end of many social invitations, you may now be in the mood to stay close to home and the incentives to move around are not strong.

13 FRIDAY
Moon Age Day 23   Moon Sign Cancer

It may not be at all easy to stay on top of things and you have to ask yourself whether it is even necessary in some cases. There might be certain issues that would be best left to their own devices, whilst you concentrate on matters that are self-evidently important. In any case your capabilities are going to be much improved later.

14 SATURDAY
Moon Age Day 24   Moon Sign Leo

A restless streak starts to become evident and ordinary, everyday tasks could be something you will run a mile to avoid. You need a change of scenery and even if you only manage to get an hour or two in your local park it could be enough to make you feel entirely different. Learn to delegate and let others do some of the work.

15 SUNDAY
Moon Age Day 25   Moon Sign Leo

Home and family seem to remain the most important consideration for you this Sunday and although friends might be urging you to do different things, many Arians will be quite happy to stay around the homestead for the moment. New incentives come along tomorrow but for the moment find a chair and sit in it.

16 MONDAY
Moon Age Day 26   Moon Sign Virgo

You should bring out your intellectual gifts now and use them for all you are worth. Half way between intuitive and inspirational you can make almost anything go your way. You will also thrive on the fact that there are several tasks to be taken on at the same time and you won't easily be thwarted by the odd setback.

17 TUESDAY
Moon Age Day 27   Moon Sign Virgo

Positive influences surround social encounters and you will be happiest when you are dealing with a number of different groups or organisations. That way when you tire of one thing you can move on to another. There is more than a little ingenuity about at present and that makes you wonderful to have around when a minor panic sets in.

18 WEDNESDAY
Moon Age Day 28   Moon Sign Libra

Communication issues could run into difficulty if you don't keep on top of them. The basic reason is that others will misunderstand what you are trying to tell them and it is therefore very important that you double-check that messages are coming across as you intend. This is more likely to be an issue at work than in social settings.

19 THURSDAY
Moon Age Day 29   Moon Sign Libra

It will probably become obvious today why things are breaking down a little. For this you can thank the lunar low, which is inclined to make you rather muddled in your thinking and actions. There is a funny side to this, however, because others find you charming and will be more than happy to smile kindly on your eccentricities.

20 FRIDAY
Moon Age Day 0   Moon Sign Libra

This is a time to get ahead by jumping the queue. Such is your charm that nobody will worry too much that you are not waiting around to be asked, and in any case this is not the way Aries acts when working at its best. In addition to having a silver tongue at present you also exhibit tremendous intuition, a gift without parallel.

21 SATURDAY
Moon Age Day 1   Moon Sign Scorpio

You demonstrate a tremendous talent for persuasion, even in situations that would have colleagues or friends baffled. For some reason people actively want to follow your lead and since they recognise that 'winner' is written through you like a stick of rock, they may well be willing to invest in you.

22 SUNDAY
Moon Age Day 2   Moon Sign Scorpio

Mental restlessness at this time could, and indeed should, incline you to abandon traditional ways of getting things done in favour of seeking out new ideas or situations. It's all about stimulation whilst present trends last and you need to feel that payback is due for all the effort you have put into life. Others find you exotic and intriguing.

23 MONDAY
Moon Age Day 3   Moon Sign Sagittarius

This might turn out to be the best time of the month to be the centre of attention. People are pleased to have you around and it will be easy for you to find the right words to impress just about anyone. You will be especially good at influencing superiors and may find yourself on the receiving end of an intriguing offer.

24 TUESDAY
Moon Age Day 4   Moon Sign Sagittarius

You may have to look again at a recent project at work and this time bring a little more ingenuity to bear on it than you did before. In affairs of the heart you could discover that normal responses won't work and that you will have to be slightly more ingenious in your approach. Pay attention to all the small details of life.

25 WEDNESDAY   *Moon Age Day 5   Moon Sign Sagittarius*

If you remain fairly committed to home and family this is mainly because of what is happening to those you love. There are new incentives for younger people and maybe a positive reversal in the health of someone who has been out of sorts for a while. A little gossip may be especially appealing to you today.

26 THURSDAY   *Moon Age Day 6   Moon Sign Capricorn*

Your mind is working fast and you might tend to express yourself in a hurried manner. No sooner do you arrive somewhere than you are on the move again and your actions might make those around you slightly dizzy. A link with the past could turn out to be quite meaningful and may cause you to think deeply.

27 FRIDAY   *Moon Age Day 7   Moon Sign Capricorn*

Family life is certain to bring out the best in you under present planetary trends. Home is the place where you bring extended entertainment and you may be planning already for an 'at home' sort of weekend to come. As the days get colder your fireside seems more welcoming but your social instincts remain strong.

28 SATURDAY   *Moon Age Day 8   Moon Sign Aquarius*

This is a marvellous time to get out into the social world – or even more likely to attract it to your own door. You do need to make new contacts and there is any number of fascinating possibilities in the pipeline. The week ahead may have positive changes in store so prepare for them now if you can.

29 SUNDAY   *Moon Age Day 9   Moon Sign Aquarius*

Planetary movements right now make you intellectually inspirational and very exciting. Many of the gains and benefits that arrive now come like a bolt from the blue and it is important to stand ready to make your move at almost any time. When you are away from work you now find it easier to relax and to make the most of family moments.

30 MONDAY
Moon Age Day 10   Moon Sign Pisces

Expect some kind of high point as far as your general plans are concerned and don't be afraid to use every skill in your armoury to get where you want to be. If this means gently nudging someone else out of the way then so be it. Worry about helping them along too once you are where you rightfully belong. You can't afford to be too sensitive today.

31 TUESDAY
Moon Age Day 11   Moon Sign Pisces

A domestic matter could prove tiresome in some way, probably mainly because there is so much you want to do out there in the wider world. Feelings may be coming to the surface and that means serious talks – something that you don't really want at the moment. Nevertheless you should take the time out to try to understand.

November
2017

1 WEDNESDAY
Moon Age Day 12   Moon Sign Pisces

Your present ability to fully enjoy life is likely to prove infectious to others and there isn't much doubt that you will be spreading your goodwill far and wide today. Aries comes across at its sunny and generous best, which means everyone loves you. This is certainly a very positive way to approach the lunar high tomorrow.

2 THURSDAY
Moon Age Day 13   Moon Sign Aries

This is likely to be one of the best days of the month for getting what you want and for being able to keep everyone else happy on the way. You won't be easily dissuaded from any course of action you want to take but since you also have what it takes to talk others round to your particular point of view all should be well.

3 FRIDAY
Moon Age Day 14   Moon Sign Aries

Things continue to look very good as far as your life is concerned and you should be registering a whole host of reasons why you can smile most of the time. Past successes become present ones, whilst you are also able to project yourself with great enthusiasm into situations that appear out of the blue. Life is on your side now.

4 SATURDAY
Moon Age Day 15   Moon Sign Taurus

Plenty of enjoyable things seem to be happening as far as your social life is concerned though personal attachments probably need more attention on your part and you could do worse than deliberately planning to sweep your partner or sweetheart off their feet in some way. Every little favour you do others today will be more than welcome.

5 SUNDAY
Moon Age Day 16   Moon Sign Taurus

Pleasure and enjoyment are high on your agenda now and you won't want to be so busy with practical issues that you fail to register the good times that are on offer. On the contrary you now have what it takes to bring a great deal of joy to even the most mundane tasks and on the way you are about as entertaining as you can be.

6 MONDAY
Moon Age Day 17   Moon Sign Gemini

Though you are quite able to bring out the best in others in social situations right now, you may be having slightly less success making them keep their heads down at work. Part of the reason lies in the fact that you are so happy-go-lucky yourself at present. In addition there are trends around indicating this to be a fairly positive time financially.

7 TUESDAY
Moon Age Day 18   Moon Sign Gemini

A trip into the past might seem to be especially rewarding at the moment and for once this could genuinely turn out to be the case for Aries. This is not because you are becoming especially nostalgic but rather because you are learning lessons as a result of happenings now long gone. It is upon such lessons that wisdom is founded.

8 WEDNESDAY
Moon Age Day 19   Moon Sign Cancer

You are still pushing forward very progressively but should heed a few words of warning with regard to finances at the moment. You are not immune to a little bad luck when it comes to almost any sort of speculation and you could lose money if you fail to think before you act. In almost every other respect, life should remain positive and happy.

9 THURSDAY
Moon Age Day 20   Moon Sign Cancer

Most aspects of life can be aided now not by what you know but rather by 'who'. Keep your eyes open for individuals who are in a position to help you out with an idea or a long-term plan for the future. There ought to be time enough today to discuss such matters and to enlist the support of individuals you like and respect.

10 FRIDAY
Moon Age Day 21   Moon Sign Leo

You are hardly likely to be waylaid by domestic chores or considerations at the moment, simply because you are so busy with the practical necessities of life. Don't be too quick to take offence when a colleague or friend seems to be critical. What they are saying is probably for your own good – even if that seems doubtful.

11 SATURDAY
Moon Age Day 22   Moon Sign Leo

A strong desire for social situations is noteworthy this weekend and whether or not you work at the weekend your mind is likely to be given over to pleasure at some stage. You will be delighted if you have a reason to paint the town red, but if not you should be able to invent one if you think hard enough.

12 SUNDAY
Moon Age Day 23   Moon Sign Virgo

You find yourself in some very enjoyable company today and will relish the cut and thrust of a busy and enjoyable time. Not everyone will want to join in the fun and games and it may be necessary to ask a few pertinent questions if someone close to you is especially quiet. Try to draw them out and to discover what is wrong.

13 MONDAY
Moon Age Day 24   Moon Sign Virgo

The necessities of life might appear to be limiting your personal freedom today but that may be only because you are holding on to issues that you could reasonably abandon right now. A fresh approach to some aspects of your life is probably necessary, together with the input of your partner or some very close friends.

14 TUESDAY
Moon Age Day 25   Moon Sign Libra

The lunar low is inclined to take the wind out of your sails now but probably not as much as would sometimes be the case. You can use the quieter tendencies that today brings in order to refuel your tanks and also for thinking ahead of yourself. Not everyone is on your side at the moment but when it matters they will be.

15 WEDNESDAY   *Moon Age Day 26   Moon Sign Libra*

Keep life as simple as possible for the moment and don't complicate issues more than strictly necessary. An uncluttered day will mean that you have more time to think up future strategies. Take time to register the fact that colleagues and friends alike are now proving to be especially helpful and make a note to return the favours later.

16 THURSDAY   *Moon Age Day 27   Moon Sign Libra*

This is an especially good time to be working in groups or with individuals you really like. Colleagues might be demanding but they ask as much of themselves as they will of you and that makes all the difference. You can't do enough at the moment for someone you really like and that could be just about everyone.

17 FRIDAY   *Moon Age Day 28   Moon Sign Scorpio*

The lunar low has passed and this is a time when you can happily see yourself in the limelight and enjoy all the accolades that are coming your way. Most of what you are doing involves subjects you understand only too well, which is why you maintain so much confidence. Only rarely will you come unstuck in conversations and these moments will be funny.

18 SATURDAY   *Moon Age Day 0   Moon Sign Scorpio*

You need to take plenty of time to make up your mind about personal matters and probably should not be taking any precipitous decisions for the moment. Let things ride and allow yourself more room to look at the broader possibilities of life. Sooner or later you will have to make choices but certainly not today.

19 SUNDAY   *Moon Age Day 1   Moon Sign Sagittarius*

Domestic matters should be turning out very much in the way you would wish, but there could be something at the back of your mind that niggles away. Perhaps you have worries about a relative or you could think that you have inadvertently upset someone? Either way the chances are that you are overplaying the situation.

20 MONDAY   *Moon Age Day 2   Moon Sign Sagittarius*

A slightly nostalgic mood could prevail today and it is likely that you would relish a less demanding role for a few hours. Wallowing in the past is not usually your thing but for once it is likely to bring out the best in you. There are also messages to be learned and some laughter over the things you did once upon a time.

21 TUESDAY   *Moon Age Day 3   Moon Sign Sagittarius*

Positive highlights appear within social and leisure interests. You should discover that your popularity is at a peak and your impressive personality is a definite boon. At work you will be more than capable and can show colleagues and superiors alike how efficient the zodiac sign of Aries can be. All attention is focused on your actions.

22 WEDNESDAY   *Moon Age Day 4   Moon Sign Capricorn*

Don't rush ahead too much with practical decisions just now. There are many options around and you will want to look at all of them before you set to a fixed course of action. This runs contrary to the usual Aries way of proceeding because you are generally inclined to act or react extremely quickly.

23 THURSDAY   *Moon Age Day 5   Moon Sign Capricorn*

Your forte right now is to make a comfortable home environment and to enjoy the quieter and less strenuous possibilities that come along during the winter months. Not that you enjoy this time of year very much. Aries is a creature of the spring and any possibility to feel the warmth of the sun somewhere else should be seriously considered.

24 FRIDAY   *Moon Age Day 6   Moon Sign Aquarius*

What a great day this would be for romance and for showing your partner just how important they are to you. If you are between relationships at the moment now is one of the best times to concentrate your efforts and to impress someone who could become quite special. Take care not to indulge too much with food and drink.

25 SATURDAY   *Moon Age Day 7   Moon Sign Aquarius*

Take full advantage of emotional links with friends and family and also spend some time today planning with others how the Christmas period is going to be handled. Someone extremely close to you could unintentionally be a great help and you make the most of all little opportunities to prove how loyal you are.

26 SUNDAY   *Moon Age Day 8   Moon Sign Aquarius*

A sense of optimism and a thirst for new ideas permeates practically everything you are doing at this stage of the month. You love being pleasant to others and what you get in return is not only affection but a great deal of practical help too. There are so many people queuing up at the moment to do you favours it could be embarrassing.

27 MONDAY   *Moon Age Day 9   Moon Sign Pisces*

Home is where you would probably prefer to be today but instead you are thrust out into an unsuspecting world. All sorts of family matters benefit from your wisdom and common sense when you are able to curl up by your own fireside, whereas more practical matters may seem to be awkward and difficult today.

28 TUESDAY   *Moon Age Day 10   Moon Sign Pisces*

Daily affairs should be more enjoyable now due to pleasant domestic influences and you should discover that loved ones have your best interests at heart. All of this makes for a pleasant sort of Tuesday but one that also demands a certain amount of effort on your part. What a great day this would be for a trip to town. Christmas shopping calls!

29 WEDNESDAY   *Moon Age Day 11   Moon Sign Aries*

Now you get the chance to take the initiative and to demonstrate how good your ideas really are. The lunar high coincides with the middle of a busy week and it is in practical and professional matters that you tend to excel. Good fortune is on your side and so you can afford to push your luck a lot more than you usually might.

30 THURSDAY
Moon Age Day 12   Moon Sign Aries

Even failure could be turned into sparkling success right now, though you need to focus all your attention in specific directions if you are to really show your worth. There is great warmth around at the moment, even though the weather is likely to be anything but warm. Your cheery smile will light up everyone's world.

December

2017

1 FRIDAY
Moon Age Day 13   Moon Sign Taurus

Your love life and romantic matters generally should be a definite high spot around now, but if this is not the case it may be that you are failing to put in sufficient effort. Also, in the everyday world, present planetary trends indicate that this would be just about the best time for getting others to back your ideas.

2 SATURDAY
Moon Age Day 14   Moon Sign Taurus

When it comes to getting on with things you may find that it can work wonders to work as a pair. You are inclined to want to group together with like-minded individuals and certainly won't be short of help when you need it the most. Your naturally warm and happy disposition begins to show through.

3 SUNDAY
☿   *Moon Age Day 15   Moon Sign Gemini*

Get out and about today – it doesn't really matter where because it's the contacts you meet along the way that are important. You may want to avoid humdrum and everyday jobs, and either leave them to others or ignore them altogether. Life itself is your best teacher at present, as you are about to discover.

4 MONDAY
☿   *Moon Age Day 16   Moon Sign Gemini*

It is very important for you to spare more than a passing thought for the feelings and sensibilities of your partner today. If you are not involved in one specific relationship at present the trends are still around but instead they may have a bearing on close family ties. Take time out to work out why others are behaving in the way they are.

149

5 TUESDAY ☿ *Moon Age Day 17   Moon Sign Cancer*

This heralds the start of a period of enjoyment and emotional fulfilment, though once again it is important that you take note of what is happening around you if you want to get the very best from these trends. One thing is more or less certain – you can get more of your own way now without having to work too hard to do so.

6 WEDNESDAY ☿ *Moon Age Day 18   Moon Sign Cancer*

You are now likely to be entering a harmonious phase in personal and romantic attachments. Working together as one of a pair is going to seem quite natural to you and even where there has been disagreement and disharmony, peace is now likely to prevail. Give some extra thought to last minute details.

7 THURSDAY ☿ *Moon Age Day 19   Moon Sign Leo*

In terms of your financial life there is now a good chance you will have to alter your plans in some way. Maybe an investment you made will cease to bring the return you would wish or it could be that you are simply re-thinking your overall strategies. There is time today to consider such matters, and incentives to do so.

8 FRIDAY ☿ *Moon Age Day 20   Moon Sign Leo*

Your personal ego is very strong at the moment and you could so easily lose your temper if others cross you about issues that you see as being your own. Before you fly off the handle, remember the time of year and just let things flow over you. Routines might seem to be quite inviting at some stage in today's proceedings.

9 SATURDAY ☿ *Moon Age Day 21   Moon Sign Virgo*

It shouldn't be difficult to get yourself into the limelight this weekend and the approach of the festive season sweeps you up in all sorts of fun activities. Whether you are with friends, colleagues or your partner, now is the time to shake free from the bonds of convention and to do something extraordinary.

10 SUNDAY ☿ *Moon Age Day 22 Moon Sign Virgo*

You are likely to delight in romantic relationships and this is a perfect day for checking out the most exciting social events and for signing yourself up to them. You certainly intend to be noticed and won't let any opportunity pass you by. The only slight downside is that there could be some fairly awkward types about.

11 MONDAY ☿ *Moon Age Day 23 Moon Sign Virgo*

Your plans and objectives could be advanced by some brand new information that comes your way. In a particularly chatty mood right now, you will also be keen to listen to what others have to say. Being nosey can sometimes work out to your advantage but it doesn't do anything for that Fire-sign Aries persona.

12 TUESDAY ☿ *Moon Age Day 24 Moon Sign Libra*

The lunar low this time around is likely to make you rather more circumspect and maybe inclined to look back, rather than projecting your ideas into the future. It won't be too much of a struggle to force yourself to take time out to do whatever takes your fancy. In any case trying too hard today and tomorrow simply won't work.

13 WEDNESDAY ☿ *Moon Age Day 25 Moon Sign Libra*

Energy and enthusiasm remains in generally short supply for now and the best way you can enjoy today is to let others do most of the work whilst you sit back and supervise. Aries can be quite good at delegation and in any case the time is probably right to let others, and especially younger people, have their moment.

14 THURSDAY ☿ *Moon Age Day 26 Moon Sign Scorpio*

You have a strong desire to make your domestic surroundings just as comfortable as can be. Loved ones have a great deal to contribute and you shouldn't belittle their contributions, even accidentally. Think before you speak and make sure to heap special praise on people who genuinely have done well of late.

15 FRIDAY ☿ *Moon Age Day 27* *Moon Sign Scorpio*

Your desire for romance should be more than fulfilled today. This trend renews and invigorates relationships and makes it possible for you to whisper those special words that mean so much to your partner. Those Arians who don't have someone special in their lives at present should look towards new possibilities.

16 SATURDAY ☿ *Moon Age Day 28* *Moon Sign Scorpio*

Minor plans start to bear real fruit and the result could be gains you hadn't really expected. For one thing you could suddenly find yourself slightly better off, though you won't have any problem spending money either. Your main concern today will be perceptive planning for the way ahead.

17 SUNDAY ☿ *Moon Age Day 29* *Moon Sign Sagittarius*

Look out for a period of advancement. It could be that you are being looked upon favourably at work or that you receive an unexpected bonus. Whatever happens today you tend to take things in your stride and react very quickly to changing circumstances. People from the past might also reappear today.

18 MONDAY ☿ *Moon Age Day 0* *Moon Sign Sagittarius*

Focus your sights on love and romance. This is where the joy resides under present trends and right now comes a certain warmth that isn't possible at other times of year. Plans should be well laid for Christmas but as usual you will want to change some of them, so be aware that this could upset family members.

19 TUESDAY ☿ *Moon Age Day 1* *Moon Sign Capricorn*

With a king-sized ego at the moment this is the time to strike out on your own and to make it plain to an unsuspecting world that you really are a typical Aries. You are likely to be energetic and may find the slight impositions brought about by the special needs of December getting in your way. Never mind, you will be festive later.

20 WEDNESDAY ☿ *Moon Age Day 2   Moon Sign Capricorn*

Today you can expect an increase in all pleasurable endeavours. It's amazing where all your present energy is coming from and you should be enjoying life to the full. New and better possibilities at work might come about as a result of someone else's slightly bad luck but you can't blame yourself for that eventuality.

21 THURSDAY ☿ *Moon Age Day 3   Moon Sign Capricorn*

Weigh up the balance between family commitments and the need to do something for yourself. If you are certain you have fulfilled your obligations then you can afford to be slightly selfish today – although others probably won't see it in that way. Don't be too influenced by your perception of the expectations of others.

22 FRIDAY ☿ *Moon Age Day 4   Moon Sign Aquarius*

You now enjoy social gatherings and also the chance to be part of a team – though there is no doubt that you still adopt a fairly dominant role. Nobody will be surprised about this because it is, after all, what is expected from Aries. At the same time you are honourable and able to admit when you are wrong.

23 SATURDAY *Moon Age Day 5   Moon Sign Aquarius*

A practical plan ought to be coming together very nicely and you won't have to look too far to find any answers you require. Friends and colleagues alike should prove to be especially helpful and it is possible that you can put something important to bed ahead of the prolonged period of festivities that lie ahead of you.

24 SUNDAY *Moon Age Day 6   Moon Sign Pisces*

Although you may not be able to express yourself quite so well today when in great gatherings of people, the same will not be true in an intimate sense. You know exactly the right words to say in order to make someone feel really good and if you are specifically looking at the possibility of making a romantic conquest do it today.

153

25 MONDAY
Moon Age Day 7   Moon Sign Pisces

Special attachments put the biggest smile on your face for Christmas Day and everything comes together in a planetary sense to offer you the best of times. Not everyone will enjoy themselves, of course, but that's Christmas. Leave the Scrooges and the miseries alone and concentrate on the fun types.

26 TUESDAY
Moon Age Day 8   Moon Sign Pisces

Widening your horizons as much as possible seems to be your thing for today. You will probably get round to looking at all those presents and there could have been something in your stocking that turns out to be especially significant. You may want to take a journey today but don't undertake it on your own.

27 WEDNESDAY
Moon Age Day 9   Moon Sign Aries

Lady Luck is about to pay you a visit, even if you don't realise it until sometime further down the line. Make this a day to remember by taking command of situations and by refusing to take no for an answer when you feel a yes in your soul. Aries is now aspiring, noble, courageous and determined. Wow! What a person you can be.

28 THURSDAY
Moon Age Day 10   Moon Sign Aries

Major endeavours and undertakings go better when you are involved and others are almost certain to realise it. This is not a time during which you will have to fight to be heard. On the contrary, people will be seeking you out because they know you always take a very positive attitude to life. Show your romantic side today.

29 FRIDAY
Moon Age Day 11   Moon Sign Taurus

Today finds you doing well in social gatherings and being the life and soul of family parties. Even on those occasions when you have to be pleasant to people you don't especially care for you will do better than you expect and the love you shower in the direction of family members is well received and returned.

30 SATURDAY   *Moon Age Day 12   Moon Sign Taurus*

Along comes a potential high spot for those of you who are working over the Christmas holidays. If you toil away in the retail trade you will be especially busy at the moment but that won't worry you with your current high energy levels. Arians who can relax today probably won't do so at all. There are bargains to be had, so get off to the shops and bag a few.

31 SUNDAY   *Moon Age Day 13   Moon Sign Gemini*

For New Year's Eve you have what it takes to adopt any kind of prominent role and will continue to be at the centre of whatever is taking place in your vicinity. This is Aries at its best and you won't be stuck for ideas, even when others are finding the going difficult. If there is any race to be won, Aries can cross the line first.

RISING SIGNS FOR ARIES

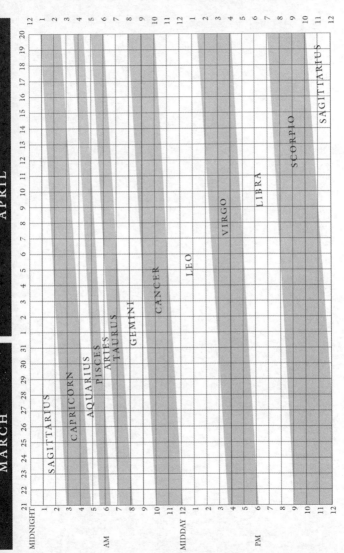

THE ZODIAC, PLANETS AND CORRESPONDENCES

The Earth revolves around the Sun once every calendar year, so when viewed from Earth the Sun appears in a different part of the sky as the year progresses. In astrology, these parts of the sky are divided into the signs of the zodiac and this means that the signs are organised in a circle. The circle begins with Aries and ends with Pisces.

Taking the zodiac sign as a starting point, astrologers then work with all the positions of planets, stars and many other factors to calculate horoscopes and birth charts and tell us what the stars have in store for us.

The table below shows the planets and Elements for each of the signs of the zodiac. Each sign belongs to one of the four Elements: Fire, Air, Earth or Water. Fire signs are creative and enthusiastic; Air signs are mentally active and thoughtful; Earth signs are constructive and practical; Water signs are emotional and have strong feelings.

It also shows the metals and gemstones associated with, or corresponding with, each sign. The correspondence is made when a metal or stone possesses properties that are held in common with a particular sign of the zodiac.

Finally, the table shows the opposite of each star sign – this is the opposite sign in the astrological circle.

Placed	Sign	Symbol	Element	Planet	Metal	Stone	Opposite
1	Aries	Ram	Fire	Mars	Iron	Bloodstone	Libra
2	Taurus	Bull	Earth	Venus	Copper	Sapphire	Scorpio
3	Gemini	Twins	Air	Mercury	Mercury	Tiger's Eye	Sagittarius
4	Cancer	Crab	Water	Moon	Silver	Pearl	Capricorn
5	Leo	Lion	Fire	Sun	Gold	Ruby	Aquarius
6	Virgo	Maiden	Earth	Mercury	Mercury	Sardonyx	Pisces
7	Libra	Scales	Air	Venus	Copper	Sapphire	Aries
8	Scorpio	Scorpion	Water	Pluto	Plutonium	Jasper	Taurus
9	Sagittarius	Archer	Fire	Jupiter	Tin	Topaz	Gemini
10	Capricorn	Goat	Earth	Saturn	Lead	Black Onyx	Cancer
11	Aquarius	Waterbearer	Air	Uranus	Uranium	Amethyst	Leo
12	Pisces	Fishes	Water	Neptune	Tin	Moonstone	Virgo